To Oliver

First published in 2010 by Conran Octopus Ltd,
a part of Octopus Publishing Group,
Endeavour House, 189 Shaftesbury Avenue,
London WC2H 8JY
www.octopusbooks.co.uk

A Hachette UK Company
www.hachette.co.uk

Distributed in the United States and Canada by
Octopus Books USA, c/o Hachette Book Group USA,
237 Park Avenue, New York, NY 10017 USA

British Library Cataloguing-in-Publication Data.
A catalogue record for this book is available from the
British Library.

Publisher: Lorraine Dickey
Managing editor: Sybella Marlow
Copy editor: Alison Wormleighton
Proofreader: Zia Mattocks
Indexer: Ingrid Lock

Art direction & design: Jonathan Christie
Picture researcher: Liz Boyd
Design assistants: Sheetal Patel, Satvir Sihota,
    Andrew Athinodorou

Production: Caroline Alberti

ISBN: 978 1 84091 543 3
ISBN: 978 1 84091 572 3 (Export edition only)

Printed in China

THE JOY OF
HOME

Naomi Cleaver

CONRAN
OCTOPUS

contents

introduction

To design a home is to design happiness, to create for ourselves a little piece of joy. In our homes, our private spaces, we can be innocent once more, uninhibited and safe. But unlike the children we once were, we, as adults, can control the space in which we live, amplifying that intoxicating combination of liberty and security to create an infinitely inspiring and comfortable home, one that can care for us and in which we can care for others: one that can make us happy.

Leading psychologist and cognitive scientist Steven Pinker has written that 'mood depends on surroundings', so it makes sense – and is even imperative – for us to shape the last four walls we see at night and those we wake up to in the morning in a way that can elicit positive emotions.

But happiness has many facets. Different things make different people happy. And different things make each of us happy in different ways, and at different times. Many of us love cream cakes but don't want to die of heart disease; I want a home that features the odd delicate piece of furniture, but also one where I can throw disco-dancing parties. Both make me happy.

The concept of conflict in happiness is one that has kept philosophers in business through the centuries. Aristotle argued that the key is to focus on a single thing that makes us happy – the disco-dancing parties, say – and pursue that above all others – so, no delicate furniture. Plato countered with the idea of harmonizing our various and varying desires to create an overarching happiness – so, disco-dancing parties plus delicate furniture that can easily be shut out of the way of frenetic dancers in boob tubes.

I think I'm with Plato on this one – I want it all and I'll settle for a degree of compromise. But the common denominator in both approaches is planning: first understanding what would make for happiness, true happiness, and then organizing life to achieve it. This can be called a design process and this is the tool to use to create the happiest of homes.

It is not so difficult. 'Every human being is a designer,' wrote Norman Potter (1923–95), interior designer, cabinetmaker, poet, tutor and, most gloriously, anarchist, in his now classic text *What is a designer*. And he was spot on. Even if you do not earn your living as a designer you are designing every day by choosing what to wear, what to eat or even where to spend your holidays. In each case you are evaluating the conditions – warm or cool day, light or hearty meal, lying on the beach or historical tour – and then constructing the best possible response to those conditions within the context of given resources. The design 'revolutionary' and entrepreneur Sir Terence Conran once described design as being irrepressibly optimistic because it is through design that we find solutions to problems, and further convert problems into opportunities.

When creating a home it is easy to confuse the process of design with the pursuit of good taste, but the two are different concepts. The chief indicator of good design is objective integrity, not subjective taste. The latter can be an unhelpful and even negative construct by which we define ourselves and judge others, salving any self-consciousness or lack of confidence in our own creativity with the emollient of what the crowd claims to be 'tasteful', equal to 'good' and therefore 'approved'.

I have seen plenty of homes that are considered 'good taste' but are bad design. They lack context, they fail to make that crucially honest and profound connection to both building and inhabitant and they end up being either bland or uncomfortably inappropriate, and ultimately dissatisfying.

Potter also said that 'design… must refer to recognizable… opportunities, or become hopelessly abstract'. It is one thing to create a pretty room set, but it is another to design an authentic home, one that is a specific and sensitive response, both harmonious and stimulating, to users, building, location and resources, all within budget and to a given timescale.

In this book you will not read instructions for how to create pretty room sets (well, maybe a few). Instead, I have written *The Joy of Home* to show how you can design your home – any home – to reflect your heart's desire, to fit in with the way you want to live, not how a floor plan or a trend wants you to, and in so doing immeasurably enhance your quality of life.

1

first things first

1

first things first

Design does not begin with a sketchpad, or even a pile of glossy interiors magazines, but with lots of questions. The more questions you ask, the more successful your design will be. In designing your home you first need to define your goals, your principal needs and desires, and the context in which those goals are to be realized – that is, the dimensions and character of your home as it is now.

THE BRIEF

Begin by making a list of what you want to achieve and the things that are important to you. To stimulate your thinking, note the positives and negatives of the way you live now – for example, 'small bathroom' or 'not enough storage' in the negatives, and 'large windows' or 'lovely garden' in the positives.

To broaden out your inquiry you could ask yourself, and those you live with, more searching questions, such as:

01

An open-plan living area is first measured out in sketch form and then translated into a scale plan. Any new design ideas can now be tested against the space available.

- ☐ What is your favourite room, and why?
- ☐ What is your least favourite room, and why?
- ☐ How do you relax, and how would you like to relax?'
- ☐ What are your interests and what would you like to be interested in?
- ☐ Do you enjoy entertaining at home? If so, how? Formal or informal?
- ☐ Do you have family and friends to stay? If not, would you like to?
- ☐ If your house were on fire, what three possessions would you grab before escaping?
- ☐ Would you describe yourself as tidy or untidy?
- ☐ What are you good at?
- ☐ What do you wish you were better at?
- ☐ What is your favourite hotel/restaurant, and why?
- ☐ What is the best thing you remember about your childhood home?

- ☐ What is your favourite place in the world, and why?
- ☐ How would you live if you were not living in the way you do now?
- ☐ What is your favourite colour?
- ☐ What is your least favourite colour?
- ☐ Do you work from home?
- ☐ Who do you live with and what are their needs?
- ☐ Who will you live with and what might be their needs? For example, are you planning to have children or do you have family or lodgers coming to live with you?
- ☐ Do you live in the country or a more urban environment?
- ☐ Do you work night shifts?
- ☐ What is your favourite climate or season?
- ☐ What is your least favourite climate or season?
- ☐ Is there a crush for the bathroom in the morning?
- ☐ Do you have difficulty sleeping?

Your responses will form your 'design brief', a document that will act as a kind of road map to the perfect home for you. And, like a road map, if you get lost or distracted (which can often happen in the midst of developing lots of different creative ideas) your design brief will get you back on track, so keep it safe.

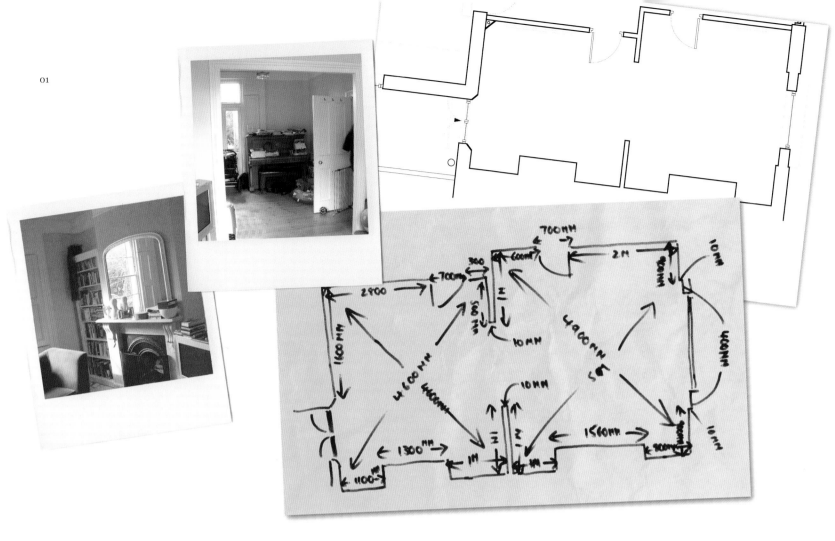

THE SURVEY

A measured survey will reveal to you just how much space, in square metres or feet, you have at your disposal. Whether you are planning new furniture or a much more thorough refurbishment, it will help you work out whether you can fit in all that you want or if you will have to prioritize, and how to do so. While you cannot expect to produce the kind of critically precise plans that a professional might produce, a home-made home survey will give you sufficiently accurate information on which to base the development of your ideas.

Many designers use laser measurers but I prefer an extra-long steel measuring tape, as this is a bit more accurate. It is useful if you have someone else to hold the other end of the tape.

1—Begin by drawing a diagram of the space you want to measure, starting with the floor (the 'plan') and then drawing each of the walls (the 'elevations').

2—When you are drawing in the perimeter of a room don't forget to include door and window openings and any recesses. It is also worth noting the location of electrical outlets and light fixtures. Ceiling-mounted light fixtures should be noted in position on your plan as if you had a bird's-eye view.

3—Do the same with the face of each wall, taking note of any mouldings.

4—Even if you are undecided about reconfiguring your layout, you should still take a note of any load-bearing walls (the solid ones that are holding up your building). If when you knock on them they sound solid and perhaps feel slightly cool, they will probably be load-bearing; if they sound hollow, they are partition walls.

5—If you are measuring up your entire home, you will need to estimate the thickness of the dividing walls and include these in your plan. If your design requires that any walls be removed, you can measure the new space after this has been done and adjust your design if necessary.

6—Now complete your diagrams with the measurements you have taken, also measuring diagonally from corner to corner across each face, as this will indicate whether the walls are square or not.

7—You are now ready to convert your diagrams into scale drawings. There are many fancy computer-aided design packages on the market that will help you do this, but you first have to learn how to use them. A more direct route is to use paper, pencil, a scale rule, a set square (carpenter's square) and a compass – plus an eraser (see pages 286–9). If this was good enough for Frank Lloyd Wright, then it's good enough for you.

STYLE

The intrinsic style of our homes can influence any design and decorative ideas we have for them, but only if we allow this to be so. Just because a home was built 200 years ago, it does not mean it needs to be designed or decorated in the style of that period. You do not dress in the fashions of the 18th century, so why would you decorate in the same way, unless you have a particular enthusiasm for that era? Equally, the fact that a home is modern does not mean it cannot be filled with antiques.

What is more important than its superficial style, and what will liberate your thinking about how to approach the design of your home, is the fundamental nature of the space. This can be described in terms of its size, rhythm, illumination, texture and scale. For example, a Georgian town house is not primarily distinguished by its mouldings, floorboards or fireplaces, but instead by the size and rhythm, or arrangement, of its windows; the height of its ceilings; the sequence of its rooms. It is down to you to choose whether you create an interior environment that harmonizes with, accentuates or contrasts with the nature of your building.

01
Both spiritually and figuratively, the heart motif is traditionally associated with the home. In this living room the designers, FAT (Fashion Architecture Taste), have interpreted this to make an ironic statement, accentuated by the reproduction fire grate set into a contemporary surround.

02
The invigorating contrast between an 18th-century drawing room and its collection of smooth, white furniture, and lighting designed in the 20th and 21st centuries serves to highlight the respective qualities in each.

2

the big idea

2

the big idea

Creativity is a gift we are all born with, a gift we express, before we can even talk, in paint and crayon, in building blocks and puréed vegetables. As we grow into adults we may fall out of the habit of using our personal brand of creativity, even in our own home. But it is here, in our domestic domain, that we can express our true creative selves most fully, and in ways that add tangible value to our quality of life. By living in a space that is redolent of our own ideas, our own creative thinking about what is good and of worth, rather than someone else's ideas, we become at one with our surroundings, building for ourselves a source of reassuring confidence and energizing self-esteem.

IDEA GENERATION

You may think you are not a 'creative person', but creativity can be taught. In design schools, students learn as much about the technique of thinking as the technology of making, and this is what you can do, too. In fact, it is an essential first step in properly resolving the issues raised by your design brief.

'Idea creativity' – the creativity involved in generating new ideas is simply the editing of information with a fresh perspective. Idea creativity is closely related to humour, and the word 'wit' embodies both. The best design ideas have both wit and insight, which stimulate pleasure.

The psychologist Abraham Maslow's signature theory is the 'hierarchy of needs', the darling of marketing strategies around the world, in which he suggests that people can only be truly 'self-actualized' – that is, fulfilling their greatest potential – if more basic needs are satisfied. In other words, you must buy that Toyota Prius so that you can be the best 'you' possible. Obviously this is not true, and I am oversimplifying to illustrate just why marketing departments are so tickled.

More useful are Maslow's observations on those happy, successful beings' creativity, which he saw as an innocent, childlike approach to the world that is 'open to experience' and 'spontaneous and expressive'. He also notes that 'creativity is more likely' in those who are 'unfrightened of the unknown, the mysterious, the puzzling'. Another feature of this creativity is integration – the unification of opposites – reminiscent of Plato's entreaty to harmonize conflicting desires to achieve the holy grail of happiness.

01
The context of location is always
a rich seam of ideas, and a carefully
observed site can provide a variety
of concepts. In this high-rise London
apartment, spaces are shaped by a
palette of light-reflective materials
and blue/grey colours, where the
inspiration is, purely and simply,
the sky right outside.

Pages 24—5
The delightfully descriptive
Soft and Hairy House by
Ushida Findlay in Japan is
indicative of the architects'
playful approach to developing
this home's concept, where
'soft' is translated as 'amorphous'
and 'hairy' is illustrated by the
lush green roof.

STIMULATING CREATIVITY

So how can we learn to be creative, to have ideas that are truly our own, that will respond to the desires and needs identified in our design brief and make for a joyful home? Here are some exercises to get the creative juices flowing.

Challenging facts

A good designer will not just accept a brief but interrogate it. I often use the 'challenging facts' technique with households who claim they need more space. By investigating what that extra space is to be used for, and analysing what space is in use already and how it is used, I can almost always apply a much more efficient solution to the use of the existing area, so that the home doesn't have to be enlarged at great expense.

Your brief may have concluded that you need a bigger bathroom. Is this actually true? Is there an alternative way of expanding the bathroom facilities?

Word association

Another psychological tool of marketing departments, but one that can also help you think in a fresh way about how to design your living space, is word association. Think of a single word that describes how you want your home to feel, and use this word to spark off your word association.

For example, if the word were 'cosy', it might go something like this: cosy – curl, feathers, bed, puppy, soft. Or if the word were 'light', the word association might be: light – shade, tree, wood, path. Or 'spacious' might produce the following: spacious – desert, quiet, nothing, peace.

Once you have identified the subsequent words, use these, not your key word, to stimulate research; investigate the different qualities of, say, softness or shade. Visit 'peaceful' places and study what makes them peaceful. Now translate your findings into ideas for your home. This technique will help you to achieve your main goal but with a great deal more character and depth. If you want your home to be full of light, for example, it need not be just a big white box with large windows but could be one that actually plays with light and animates space, in the way that the sun falls through a leafy tree.

Word association can also serve to interrogate the motivation behind your key word. By following this exercise you may discover an entirely new, even opposite, approach to the atmosphere you want to create.

01

If there's one thing I can't bear to be without it is my sketchbook, where I can record all my ideas, develop concepts and 'scrapbook'.

02

Without the sculptural ceiling feature, the architecture of this home could justifiably be described as a frigid, white box. To inject some sensuality, intimacy and individuality, an analogy has been drawn with stalactites to create a suspended ceiling like no other.

The test of ten ideas in ten minutes, or thereabouts

This exercise is related to word association and especially the psychiatrist Carl Jung's study of the time delay between responses in the successive articulation of words or ideas. Jung found that the greater the delay between our responses, the less honest they are. Given that the aim is to expose our unique 'creative DNA', a very limited timeframe is essential. In this way there is little escape from the truth.

This technique also helps to purge you of what designers sometimes call 'primary generators'. These are those first ideas we all have that may not actually be the right ones or may simply be clichés, but can be ever-present. If you do not exorcise them in the beginning, they can act as obstacles to a much better solution.

Take your design challenge – perhaps something as simple as a new cooking zone – and sketch out your ten ideas in ten minutes. They may be ideas for the layout, for the atmosphere or for something else entirely: see what you come up with. It may result in lots of questions, which should be enjoyable as well as productive to research. Try the technique as many times as you feel is useful. To develop creativity, you have to work at it.

A is for analogy

Drawing on analogous situations can be invaluable in generating a new way of looking at a problem and devising a solution. Perhaps your problem is storage in a tight space, in which case it can be helpful to look at nature's storage solutions. In a honeycomb, for example, contiguous cells allow for a great deal of storage in often oddly shaped, confined spaces. Nature is a treasure trove of tried and tested design solutions, so a rich source of analogies.

Wishful thinking

Indulging in some wishful thinking can liberate your thoughts to reveal unbridled desires. You may be surprised to discover just how achievable your dream home is, so long as you dare to dream it.

Not thinking

Sometimes, after you have worked so hard at trying to solve a problem by coming up with a design, but to no avail, the perfect idea will just come along when you are least expecting it. Being creative is hard work... plus tea breaks.

The sketchbook

Record all your ideas in a sketchbook. I maintain two: one large-format and one smaller one that I can carry around with me. Both are full of rough drawings, notes and scraps, from newspaper images to sugar packets.

01

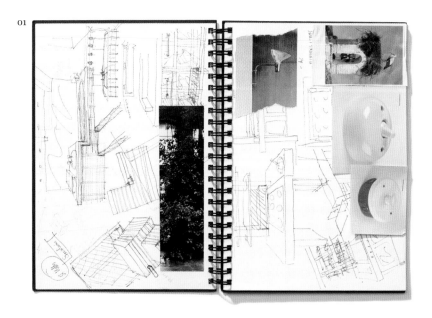

Two kinds of rhythm are at play here. Repetitive rhythm is expressed in four elements: the collection of pendant lights; the two Panton chairs; the tessellated shelving and the checkered flooring.

There is then transitional rhythm to be discerned between these four elements, since you will no doubt find your gaze is drawn through the space and toward whatever might exist beyond the windows.

01

THE DESIGNER'S TOY BOX

I am often asked what the 'rules of design' are, but the fact is, when it comes to ideas, there are no rules, because the allure of artistry is so subjective. Instead, there is a series of well-established observations of how we experience our surroundings, observations that I have called 'toys'. This is because they are to be played with, either emulated or subverted – with the exception of access and safety. Use the 'toy box' as a way of evaluating your ideas.

Sizing up

The magic in math is revealed in proportion and scale. Proportion is the ratio of one element to another or of one element to the whole; scale describes the ratio between the size of two objects.

Leonardo Fibonacci, perhaps the greatest mathematician of the Middle Ages, not only introduced Arabic numerals to Europe, replacing Roman numerals, but also codified the proportions that spontaneously occur in nature into a mathematical sequence (0, 1, 1, 2, 3, 5, 8, 13,...), in which any number in the sequence is the sum of the previous two. Known as the Fibonacci sequence, it approximates to the ancient and mysteriously compelling architectural device of the 'golden section'. This is where a line is divided into two unequal parts in which the ratio of the larger part to the smaller one is the same as the ratio of the whole line (that is, the sum of the two parts) to the larger part.

A golden rectangle has the short and long sides in this very same proportion.

The golden ratio is as vivid in the spiralling scales of a pineapple as in the facade of the Parthenon and even in our own bodies, a fact that was interpreted during the Renaissance as having great spiritual significance. Leonardo da Vinci's famous drawing of 'ideal man' illustrates the concept by echoing a pentagram, which is another geometrical expression of the golden section.

The 20th-century architect Le Corbusier employed the golden section and Fibonacci numbers to create his signature method of proportioning and scale known as Le Modulor, two sets of measurements that relate directly to the size of a man: one set relates to the height and the other to the height including an upstretched arm.

Le Corbusier applied these to his Unité d'habitation apartment building in Marseilles with varying degrees of success. While the building makes a powerful impression outside, inside it the ceiling heights feel cramped because they equate to the height of his Modulor man with arm upstretched. This neatly illustrates Le Corbusier's enormous ego. Nevertheless, proportioning living space with specific regard to the proportions of the human body can be both logical and emotionally powerful.

Rhythm without blues

Rhythm can load a space with stimulating energy in the same way it does music, through repetition, progression, transition and opposition.

- Repetition is pretty self-explanatory, referring to an element being repeated.
- Progression is where a characteristic of an element is progressively amplified or reduced, a typical example being size.
- A transitional rhythm is one that gently leads the eye from one space to another.
- Oppositional rhythm is the rhythm of contrasts, through which contrasting elements can exaggerate respective qualities. For example, a space with a low ceiling next to a space with a high ceiling will magnify the effect of the volume of each. Note that adjacent elements that do not significantly contrast, but are not quite the same either, will usually result in mediocrity.

Balance – and the lack of it

The concept of balance in a space is expressed in symmetry, and variations thereof. We are instinctively drawn to symmetry because, in nature, symmetry suggests blooming health and, more importantly, fertility. While the use of symmetry in your home will not necessarily make you more fertile, it will add innate appeal. The duplication of elements on either side of a given line creates symmetry, or if it is around a central point it is known as radial symmetry.

Asymmetry – the absence of symmetry – gives a space contemporary dissonance, putting me in mind of what the Chinese businesswoman and patron of architecture Zhang Xin once said: 'It is easy to fall in love with what is conceived to be right and proper, good and beautiful, but the chief task of new architecture is to disturb that sense of comfort.' For 'architecture' read 'design' while considering this provocative idea.

Fresh perspectives

Perspective is the way in which we perceive depth. Manipulate perspective and you manipulate the perception of depth and therefore space. Illustrating this phenomenon perfectly, the distorted room known as an Ames Room was devised in 1934 by an American ophthalmologist. Although the room had a trapezoidal shape, a sloping ceiling and floor, and walls that slanted outward, it looked cube-shaped when viewed from a peephole at the front. From this viewing point, it made a small child standing in one rear corner appear to be the same size as a man standing in the other rear corner.

While a sloping floor might be somewhat impractical, exaggerating the size of elements close to the main viewing point compared with those farther away will increase a sense of depth. Effects can be tested with a simple model – see 'What will it look like?', page 46.

Distraction

The concept of distraction can be very useful in situations where, for whatever reason, it is not possible to change less attractive elements. For example, a dramatic feature can draw the eye away from unappealing imperfections.

Integrity, the new taste

Designers often talk of the value of integrity in a design. This is because integrity indicates 'rightness' and expresses the value of context, the midwife of good design. An idea or design with integrity will be honest, it will bear scrutiny and it can be proven not to be fake or, if it is, it will be couched in wit, equating to insight and humour.

I once filmed in a home built in the 1960s in which the owners had installed an inglenook fireplace. As a result, the home lacked design integrity. However, it might have had it if the obvious aesthetic and even spiritual conflicts between a bland 1960s house and a fireplace harking back to the 16th century had been acknowledged with a degree of wit, transforming reductive ersatz into amusing kitsch. Well, almost.

Essential elegance

In design and decor the word 'elegance' is often used in place of 'good taste', though it can be applied to opulence as much as that which is impressively restrained. However, the restrained approach is more valuable to a successful design process and, I feel, more compelling in the final result.

The perfection of imperfection and the luxury of what seems simple

All flawless homes resemble each other, but each flawed home is flawed in its own way (with apologies to Tolstoy). The imperfections in our homes can characterize them, and can literally mark them out, more so than sometimes sanitizing faultlessness.

The Japanese have always cherished what in the Western world might be seen as imperfections. They call this kind of beauty *wabi-sabi*, which describes the beauty in places that are too often overlooked – beauty that can also be transitory, eliciting melancholy and poetic longing. The 20th-century Japanese author Jun'ichiro Tanizaki refers to this very idea when he writes: 'While we do sometimes use silver for... sake cups, we prefer not to polish it. On the contrary, we begin to enjoy it only when the lustre has worn off, when it has begun to take on a dark, smoky patina.' If luxury is that which is rare or difficult to achieve, then, interestingly, this concept of *wabi-sabi* can fundamentally reframe what in the Western world has historically been perceived as luxurious.

Intimacy needs privacy

Primitive man's ideal landscape was the savannah – open space that exposed danger, plus the odd low tree or thicket to provide protection. Correspondingly, open-plan homes, balanced by cosy corners in which we can hide away, will have a visceral appeal, as well as offering a seductive sense of intimacy.

The deity in the details

While it is unwise to work on details amid the flurry of first ideas, as this can sometimes obstruct the creative flow, the way in which elements meet, or are fixed in place, will inevitably influence the look and feel of your home, whether it is bijou or simply big. Once you have established the key components, apply as much energy and focus to finessing the finer points so that they complement, instead of compromise, the overall impression.

Don't be afraid of the dark

Seasonal Affective Disorder, or SAD, is the gloomy mood produced by gloomy weather: without enough light we can become depressed. This is why most of us want our homes to be filled with light. But in pursuing this we may miss out on amplifying the effects of light by contrasting it with darkness, and by introducing shadows that bring light alive.

In the far north of Finland, the celebrated architect and theorist Juhani Pallasmaa, notes how 'homogenous bright light paralyses the imagination...' and admires architectural spaces '...where there is a constant, deep breathing of shadow and light.' Far south in Japan, Jun'ichiro Tanizaki describes in *In Praise of Shadows* 'shadows that formed... a quality of mystery and depth superior to that of any painting or ornament.' Darkness can dramatize space by dissolving boundaries. It replaces what can be seen with the eye with what can be seen only with the mind's eye.

01
The combination of a shaded garden and small, leaded peripheral windows would limit the amount of daylight penetrating this living room, so instead of deploying decorating tricks to make the space brighter the owners have embraced the dusky mood, where it is pale furnishings and fittings that serve as punctuating beacons of light.

02
Commonplace materials and the simple form of this kitchen are made special by the handcrafted chisel detail on the edges of the structural elements.

The beauty of quiet abundance is resonant in a collection of clay pots, each unique while subscribing to the collections' overriding characteristics of material, shape, scale and colour palette, a palette that is echoed in the furnishings. Perhaps most impressive, though, is the high-relief sculpture of ancient violence mounted above, where the significant degree of contrast between the large scale of the sculpture and the relatively small scale and density of the pots makes this combination of two quite different 'displays' work.

The curse of coordination

Overt, or contrived, consistency creates bland, superficial spaces. Think, for example, of the majority of show homes and their 'accent' colours. On the other hand, covert, subtle echoing of meaningful themes is pleasing: we human beings intuitively and actively seek out patterns.

The art of display

The Enlightenment was not just an age of revolution in Western political, philosophical and religious thought. It also launched a whole new display craze: this was the cabinet of curiosities. In such a cabinet the intellectual occupations of the homeowner were laid bare, usually featuring objects from 'the natural world', such as fossils and exotic shells. To some degree the same motivation can be said to apply to the display of objects in our homes today, be they knick-knacks or paintings, sculpture or plants.

- Small-scale items will make the most impact when grouped with other items (hence 'the cabinet'), either of the same size or larger, especially when the grouping is informed by shared characteristics, say colour or texture.
- Larger items that you wish to display independently should have sufficient personality to justify such prominence, or it will look like they are simply waiting to be shut away.
- When displayed against strongly patterned backgrounds, objects need to win the battle for attention or they will get lost, so use dramatic pieces only. Paintings or drawings can be given deep mounts to avoid visual confusion. Spotlighting can help draw attention to pieces and make backgrounds recede.
- While accessories and plants are not usually fixed in place, pictures often are. The best way to mount a collection of pictures is to set the arrangement out on the floor first, then mark out positions in pencil on the wall before hanging in place.
- I always find that odd-numbered collections of items make for a more stimulating effect, while even numbers infer formality.

Soundscape

Much has been written in the field of architecture about the relationship between sound and space. The shape and consistency of a building inform its sound, and sound can influence our perception of a building.

On the smaller scale of a home, what can be usefully gleaned from these studies is that a predominance of hard surfaces will make a space echo, and perhaps feel larger than it really is, though it will be quite noisy. Soft or textured, rounded or inclined surfaces will dampen sound, not only making a space quieter but also making it feel more intimate – though bear in mind that the complete absence of sound can often become disconcerting.

Touchy-feely

Touch is the immediate interface between our skin and our homes, yet we tend to think of the value of touch only when considering upholstery or soft furnishings. The way a space feels can shape our impression of it just as much as how it looks. There is the satisfying abrasiveness of coir matting on bare feet; the caress of an upholstered wall as we brush past; the indented roundness of an aged, brass door knob in our hand; the coolness of handmade tiles against the roughness of their edges. By bringing alive our senses in this way, our homes themselves come alive and engage with us on a profoundly sensual level.

01

Delicious

It may seem odd when developing your designs to think of the way a home might smell or taste, but smell can be therapeutic. One of the chief tasks in the design of a home is usually to avoid bad smells, such as those from recycled rubber flooring or new carpet with a synthetic backing. But because smell is a distinguishing characteristic of a home, there is a case for actively 'designing in' contributions to the scent of home.

The use of aromatic woods, such as cedar, is one obvious method, and I am always drawn to the damp-straw scent of rush matting. It is even possible to buy scented paints, though I would be wary of synthetically perfumed elements: the key to scenting a home is subtlety. And health.

The taste of a home (as opposed to the taste in a home) is a purely abstract concept, unless you have some odd cravings, but it is still one worthy of contemplation. Something does not need to be edible to make us salivate.

02

01, 02 and 03
A landscape painting by artist
Kurt Jackson (01), bursting
with colour both bold and
subtle, is distilled into a colour
palette (02) made manifest in
this living room (03).

01

02

Colour your home beautiful

One of the first design projects I was set at college concerned the assembly of small, wooden cubes, which we were instructed to paint in different ways to express the science of colour: primaries, secondaries, complementaries, hues, shades, tints, tones. And how we all hated it. If there is one way to turn a person off colour, this is it.

What makes colour compelling is not its science but its romance, its emotional resonance. And to learn about this you can do no better than to study really good paintings or photography – or make your own, especially of Mother Nature, whose sense of colour is matchless.

A helpful exercise is to distil an image that you find particularly powerful into a colour palette. Do this with several images and you will see a pattern emerge. Use these in your home, as they are the colours with which you have a meaningful connection.

A little knowledge of the science of colour can then help you to develop your colour scheme(s). Note as follows:

☐ Primary colours are red, blue and yellow.
☐ Secondary colours are purple, green and orange.
☐ Complementary colours are yellows and purples; greens and reds; oranges and blues.

☐ A hue describes the pure characteristic of the colour, such as red or orange.
☐ A shade is a hue with black added.
☐ A tint is a hue with white added.
☐ A tone is a hue with grey added.

Life's rich

Dense pattern and texture can add voluptuous intensity to a space, while very open patterns can give depth and the impression of continuity. Patterns and textures can be mixed together, but to avoid chaos you will need to create a hierarchy, where it is clear who the 'daddy' is. Success will also rely on the mix sharing a framework of motifs, such as colour or shape.

01

The curves and colour employed
in this space recall the embryonic
environment, our first ever home.

02

Angular sections are carved out
of these curved walls, striking a
balance between intuitive comfort
and essential practicality.

Curvaliscious

The homes of creatures other than humans are always curved: nests, burrows, bowers. This has led some to argue that curved lines in habitable space are more natural to us, though this presupposes that man, who just happens to be able to create straight lines as well as curved ones, is not part of nature. A less contentious characterization of rounded space is organic, where curves suggest that a space is integrated with its surroundings, where the sinuous fluidity of a curve is the opposite to the finality of a straight line. Back to the contentious: curved and rounded shapes can also be perceived as feminine, as invitational and seductive, and this is why the curve is often used in retail environments.

In reality, while technology is allowing for more curvy architecture and objects in our lives, building curved walls or even ceilings is an expensive business. Tight budgets prefer straight lines; and the fewer corners and curves, the better.

However, such considerations do not stop you from introducing less expensive curved objects into your home, such as furniture or lighting. These will refract sound and light in the same way as a curved wall.

02

This celebrated home of a
wheelchair-bound owner consisting
of floors that can rise and fall
designed by Dutch architect
Rem Koolhaas, is a masterclass in
silver linings, where challenges are
realized as opportunities for bold,
dramatic design concepts.

01

Access all areas

Universal Design is concerned with making all spaces accessible to all. This principally refers to wheelchair users. If you are designing a home in which a wheelchair needs to be used, note that 800mm (31½in) is considered the minimum width for a doorway. You will also need to do the following:

- Consider the height of every feature such as light switches, countertops, tables and sinks as well as ensuring there is nothing below things like countertops, so that a wheelchair can slip in underneath.
- Think about how a wheelchair user will best be able to move from the wheelchair into, for example, a shower or a bed. This usually necessitates grab rails and an adjacent seat, depending on the degree of physical impairment.

This is quite a specialist field and government organizations and charities will be able to help you design all the necessary details into your home, but do remember it need not look like a hospital. Non-standard heights and widths, essential smooth floor surfaces, and wet rooms can be very glamorous.

Orientation

When deciding where to spend what time where, and in what occupation, do bear in mind the orientation of your home: a southwest-facing aspect will be in direct sun from around midday until the sun sets in the west, while a northeast-facing aspect will only benefit from the sun in the early morning, when the sun rises.

Safety first... and last

In the design of your home, safety will be bound by building regulations and common sense can fill in any gaps. All of the following precautions are strongly recommended:

- If occupants are unsteady on their feet, ensure there are no errant floor surfaces such as slippery rugs or variations in level.
- Install nonslip flooring in a bathing area and perhaps nonslip treatments in the bathtub.
- Install thermostatic controls to taps (faucets) and showers to avoid scalding.
- Avoid loose cables and cords.
- Install smoke detectors and carbon-monoxide detectors.
- Keep a fire extinguisher to hand.

If you have young children you will also need to do the following:

- Install a safety gate at the top of any flights of stairs (this need not be as ugly as they often are – you could have one made to match your staircase)
- Secure waste bins.
- Fit drawer latches and locks, especially on cupboards and drawers that contain harmful objects and substances. You may also want to consider oven and dishwasher locks. And arrange the hob (cooktop) so it is out of reach.
- Fit covers on electrical outlets.
- Fit window guards on accessible windows.
- Avoid any furniture that could be tipped over.
- Guard open fires.
- Protect machines, such as a DVD player, from foreign objects being deposited in them, including small hands.

But do not overdo it. Children do not stay small and vulnerable for long. It has also been scientifically proved that children need some risk in their lives so that they can learn about the world they live in.

WHAT WILL IT LOOK LIKE?

Using your imagination to conceive design ideas costs nothing, at least in terms of hard cash. Implementing those ideas, on the other hand, can represent a significant investment. And, of course, the more imaginative the ideas, the higher the risk of failure, as well as the greater the potential for joy – such is the curse of creativity.

This is why it is important to guard against what could be expensive mistakes by accurately depicting how a proposed scheme is going to look and feel. You need to 'test' the pictures in your head as much as possible before committing the time and money required to realize them.

In the larger hotels and hotel chains it is a salutary convention, when developing new designs for guest rooms, to first build a prototype room, now fashionably known as a 'room lab'. In this way previously untried ideas, principally in technology but also in decor, can be thoroughly evaluated and refined, or rejected, before a new concept is implemented, usually many times over. Such elaborate experimentation in pursuit of perfection is unfortunately not realistic when designing the private home, but there are other, more accessible techniques available.

Sampling

It is a matter of common sense to see, touch, even smell something that you not only plan to commit money to, but also intend to live with. What sampling allows you to do is to view the relationships between finishes, and also between the larger objects, in a given space and at different times of day.

Finishes

The revelations wrought by assembling samples of every finish you are considering for a space cannot be overestimated. You may be surprised to see how different some materials – especially those that obviously react to light, such as shiny ceramic or shimmering silk – can look, according to the illumination in the space for which they are destined.

Happily, suppliers will give you samples of most materials free of charge – from timber to tile, and from glass to stone. When it comes to wallpaper and fabric, many suppliers will have 'jumbo'-sized samples available to loan. This can be invaluable, especially when a large pattern or natural material is involved.

If you find it difficult to assemble all your samples, do not be shy about taking samples you can source into showrooms featuring those you cannot. For example, take a floor tile into a kitchen showroom.

The most common form of sampling is to paint small areas of a proposed colour onto the intended wall or other surface. If you are nervous about this, paint a sheet of paper or board and attach this to the wall, or better still a cardboard box as this will show you how the same colour can look so different on adjacent planes.

The best way to mount loose samples is on large pieces of foam board, one for each space. Ideally accompany them with a drawing and/or photograph of the space.

MODELLING

Objects

As regards objects such as freestanding furniture, lighting and accessories, it can be extremely helpful to be able to borrow some of the items you have in mind from suppliers and try them out before making a purchase. This is no longer the convention it once was, so you may need to negotiate mutually satisfactory terms. For example, you may be allowed to purchase items on the understanding that if they are not suitable you will be able to return them for a full refund, so long as they are in the condition in which they were sold in the first place.

If you are considering bespoke features, such as built-ins, it can be a very instructive exercise to invest in the sampling of certain key details at full scale. This process is particularly useful if you are considering expensive or innovative features.

Most professional design studios employ sophisticated computer modelling or commission specialist model-makers to realize their schemes in Lilliputian glory. But there are simpler methods.

The David Hicks trick

This method of mini model-making is typical of the debonair energy of the 20th-century interior designer David Hicks.
1 — Take a long strip of paper and fold it into as many planes as there are walls.
2 — Draw the elevations of your proposed design for each wall on to each of the sequential paper 'walls'.
3 — Assemble, with cellophane tape, into your model room for review.

Easy scale model

1 — Paste your scale plans and elevations onto foam board (the thinner the better and available from all good art supplies stores).
2 — Using a scalpel (10A blades are best, again available from all good art supplies stores) and a cutting mat, cut out walls, floors and ceilings, complete with doorways and windows.
3 — Assemble with glue.

4 — If you are now feeling confident, try modelling the features within your space – from dividing walls to a kitchen island or furniture – by printing and pasting onto foam board a plan and a set of elevations for each of the features. Cut out and assemble with glue, and place in your model space.

Full scale ahead

With this method you are working at full scale (1:1) – in other words, life size. It is particularly useful for assessing the relationship between potential planes and objects.
1 — Mark the floor of the space you are redesigning, to indicate proposed features, such as dividing walls, built-ins and furniture. Chalk and spray paint can be used on floors destined for re-covering, or string and pins on those that will not be re-covered.
2 — Cut discarded cardboard boxes to size and use parcel tape to shape the mass of the components in your proposed design.
3 — At full scale you can also test a lighting scheme consisting of floor and table lamps, simply by using lamps you already own to emulate the effect of the new ones you are considering.

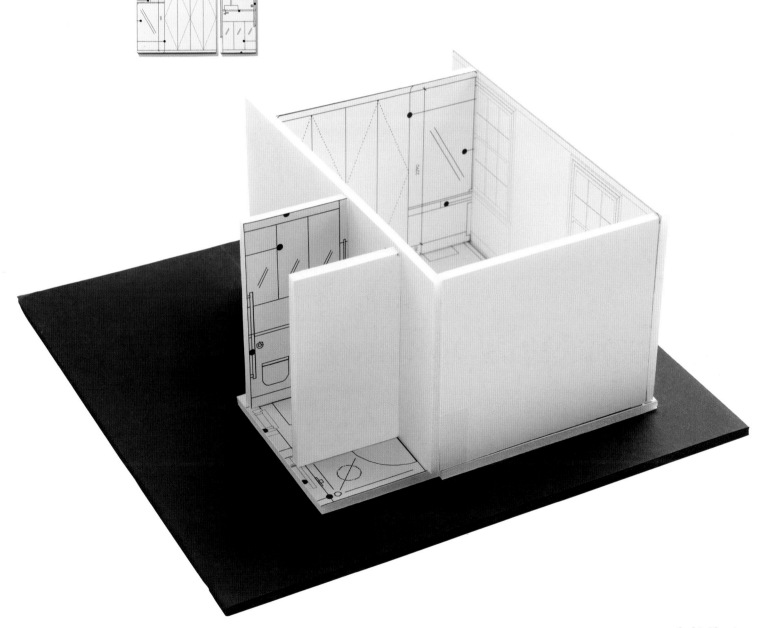

Opposite
A David Hicks-style sketch model, where walls are sketched onto a strip of paper and folded into a little paper 'room'.

Left
Here, scale drawings of walls and floors have been pasted onto foam board and cut out ready to be assembled.

Below
Once assembled, the scale and proportion in the design proposal for a master bedroom and adjoining shower room can be properly evaluated.

ILLUSTRATION

'Rendering' is how architects and designers describe what could also be called 'colouring in' – vivifying scale drawings with tint and tone. Prior to the advent of computer-aided design (CAD) this was always done by hand. The 20th-century Venetian architect and interior designer Carlo Scarpa is celebrated for his beautiful drawings as much as for his architecture.

Interestingly Scarpa rarely produced perspective drawings, which are arguably the most communicative format. Perhaps this is because drawing in perspective is difficult to master, either by hand or by computer. Architects and interior designers, cognizant of their limitations in both skill and time available for a project, refer the production of perspective drawings to specialists, particularly if what is required is a startlingly vivid CAD 'walk-through'.

Thanks to digital photography and the proliferation of personal computers and printers that can also operate as scanners and photocopiers, there are ways to assume an approximation of these skills instantly, often with more soulful results. (If you do not have access to this equipment, there are always copy shops.)

HOW TO CHEAT AT PERSPECTIVE DRAWING

Method A

1 — Take a photograph (or paste photographs side by side to form one composite image) of the space you are redesigning. This image needs to be fairly large – say A3, or 210 x 297mm ($8\frac{1}{4}$ x $11\frac{3}{4}$in) – so print it out at this size, or print it small and enlarge it on a photocopier.

2 — On a sheet of tracing paper the same size as your enlarged photographic image, trace the image picking out only those features that will remain in your intended scheme. If you are just redecorating, this will consist of the outline of the entire room. If yours is a major refurbishment you may end up with only a few lines, which are just guidelines at that.

3 — Download from the internet or take your own photographs of the objects, finishes (these can also be scanned) and even details you intend for your scheme. Enlarge these so they are in proportion to the space in your main image, and print them out. It is helpful, too, if the images of the objects are roughly from the same viewpoint as the photograph of the space for which they are intended, though total accuracy is not necessary. The aim of this exercise is to test the relationships between all your prospective components, not win the local art prize (though you never know).

4 — If you are planning a major refurbishment you will now need to complete the outline of the planned space. The guidelines you traced from the existing space will help. The general rule of thumb is to draw new lines parallel to old, which allows you to retain some semblance of a convincing perspective.

5 — You can now 'virtually' decorate your space. Apply the images of your proposed objects and finishes to create a collage, which you can then complete with paint, coloured pencils or pastels.

6 — Don't forget sources of natural and artificial light, which can be represented with a localized wash of white paint. Spaces can look very different through the day, depending on the arc of the sun and the location of windows. This is even more the case at night, when artificial light is the only source of illumination.

Method B

1 — Follow the method to build an 'easy scale model' (see page 48).

2 — Photograph your model, printing the final image out to the same size as in method A, step 1, and proceed from method A, step 3.

3 — You can approximate the effect of natural light by placing a source at your model windows or glazed doors before photographing.

If at first you don't succeed…

After you have assembled your sample boards, models and perspective drawings, if you do not like the result, list the reasons why you feel your design does not work. Now start again, comforted by the fact that you have saved yourself from investing in something you now realize you could not live with. The best designers rarely cling to their first ideas.

This page
Here, I took a photograph of the space to be redesigned in a client's home and traced the structural elements I planned to retain in my projected design proposal. I then pasted the resulting sheet of tracing paper to a sheet of black paper and used a white pencil to illustrate my design.

3
decor recipes

3
decor recipes

The most satisfying kind of home is the one that expresses your personal brand of creativity while capitalizing on your building's architectural good points – as well as one that, in practical terms, works. Making your home work is a matter of cool logic – a mainly 'left brain' endeavour that will calculate the appropriate amount of clearance required in a galley kitchen, for example.

Engaging the intuitive 'right brain' to produce an individually comforting and inspiring home can be a far trickier challenge. This is because original creative ideas can take more time: time to think, time to look around, time to experiment, and then time to do the same thing all over again, until you come up with an idea you are happy with, especially if you are a more 'left brained' kind of person.

In designing a home this process might seem intolerably ponderous – and expensive, too. Painting a picture requires just paint and canvas; decorating the living room requires a bit more.

If time or inspiration is short, it can be useful to look at what others have successfully achieved in similar circumstances. But to avoid simply duplicating someone else's ideas and, as a result, suffocating your own, the trick is to objectively distil features into characteristics and principles, observing what works where and how.

You may be surprised to discover that there are a limited number of common themes in decor, albeit with infinite interpretations, which can produce a confidence-building road map to a creatively rewarding home. An analogy can be drawn with literature: the British critic Christopher Booker has argued that there are only seven stories in the world – tragedy (*Macbeth*); comedy (*Pride and Prejudice*); overcoming the monster (*Jaws*); voyage and return (*Alice in Wonderland*); quest (*The Lord of the Rings*); rags to riches (*Cinderella*) and rebirth (*A Christmas Carol*), again with infinite interpretations. Such an argument does not cynically refute original creativity but speaks of common human experience.

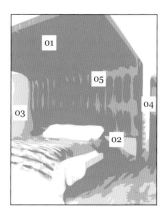

architectural

The enduring legacy of the Austrian architect Adolf Loos rests in his article of 1908 entitled 'Ornament and Crime'. In it Loos famously argues that ornament is a slave to capricious fashion, resulting in an immoral waste of resources. Inflammatory at the time, especially in the face of the highly decorative Art Nouveau movement and its cousin, the Vienna Secession, Loos's arguments still sound fairly bad-tempered. But he has a good point, which is why his words have endured and why they resound in the interiors of today.

These spaces could collectively be described as architectural. The decorative style rests not in furnishings and accessories but in what architects and designers call 'the envelope' – walls, ceilings, floors and even windows and doors.

Materials are consequently selected for their structural potential in combination with notable texture and neutral colour: shuttered concrete, glossy composites, figured timber, stone. All other elements – freestanding furniture, lighting, accessories – not only are minimal in number but also echo the characteristics of the architectural finishes. Invisible, fitted furniture is also essential.

key ingredients

01
A restricted material palette. The bed canopy is sculpted from timber, as is the floor. The only other material in evidence is the wall finish and the material from which the bedside lights are made (except, of course, for the bedding).

02
Limited elements and the benefits of integration. This bedroom consists of just five elements: walls, floor, bed, canopy and side lights; bedside tables or night stands are integrated into the canopy form.

03
Seamlessness. The detailing in the few elements there are is minimal, and consists almost entirely of smooth and seamless planes.

04
Size. Generous scale is often a requisite of a successful 'architectural' decorative style, creating drama and interest with self-limiting components.

05
Sculptural qualities. The sinuous form and sheer size of this bed canopy makes an unambiguous sculptural statement.

02

architectural

01
Concrete panels, picture windows and Modernist furniture all conspire to create an architectural style.

02
The elemental beauty in the unrefined materials and textures of a building site is evident here in the exposed brick, painted a chic matte black. Combined with a lightly polished concrete floor, minimal stainless-steel kitchen and simple dining furniture, the look is completed by chunky raw steel window frames.

03
A concrete 'shell' is divided by an almost imperceptible glass sheet to delineate this living space.

03

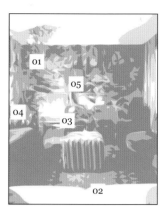

camp

Camp is theatrical. It exaggerates to amuse both inhabitant and visitor. Extrovert spectacle is the main goal here. Saturated colour; texture, pattern and objects at large scale – from lighting to statuary – and exotica, from religious icons to animal skins, exemplify camp decor, usually pulled together by a consistent colour palette. The rule appears to be 'more will never be enough', but the effectiveness of camp lies in careful selection and considered display, so that the great deal of effort that has gone into choosing provocative furnishings and accessories is not wasted. Lights, camera, action.

key ingredients

01
Theatre. A dramatic, life-size mural of a sylvan glade is the suspend-your-disbelief moment in this room, inviting you to scramble up the rocks at the side of a woodland stream. The saccharine mural is pregnant with irony, because it is, of course, a wall, and its use in the decor here is entirely cognisant of that fact: this is the ironic bit.

02
Bold colour. Not all rooms described as camp feature bold colour, but many do, and here those colours are bright green, bright yellow and bright red, which is one bold palette.

03
The discipline of display. The use of symmetry binds otherwise discordant themes together.

04
Pattern and texture. This space features a theatrical combination of big patterns and textures, but all of these seemingly disparate pieces work together because they subscribe to the same overriding palette within the context of a square furniture plan.

05
Layering. A concept often used in fashion, which can equally be applied to the home, where layering of different elements can create the theatre that characterizes camp. Here carefully chosen paintings are provocatively 'layered' on top of the biggest picture in the room, the mural.

camp

01

Textured gold walls; a baroque-style (though plastic) mirror frame; a minimal sink and a highly stylized tap (faucet) claim the glittering camp crown in this bathroom.

02

The dominant chandelier combined with baroque and ethnic pieces are what put this dining room in the camp category.

03

The style of Barbara Hulanicki, founder of iconic fashion boutique Biba in the 1960s, could arguably be described as camp. In her own apartment silver leather furniture and playful accessories create an atmosphere of kitsch cool.

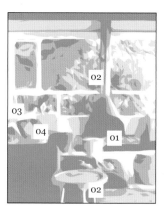

comfortable

The comfortable home is the generous home, enfolding and forgiving. There is a tangible feeling of cosseting, invitation and accessibility.

To create this style, choose materials that improve with rough treatment – and may even look as if they've had some already – such as wood or metal. Likewise textiles, which should be antique or second-hand. Scale is important, as decor needs to be big enough to embrace, and substantial enough to take wear and tear... and to look better for it. Slipcovers that can be easily washed play a significant role, as does an abundance of personal mementoes.

Seating is well padded, strewn with patterned or textured cushions and throws that will mask the marks of use. Rooms are punctuated with oversized bowls of near-wild flowers. Design decisions are not binary – old/new, simple/complex, dark/light, machined/handmade, bright/neutral – for ease is the priority. Comfortable homes make you feel that if you spilled or broke something, it wouldn't matter too much, and might even add value.

key ingredients

01
Hygge. *Hygge* is a Danish word for which there is no English translation. The closest we can get is 'cosy' but *hygge* also means having a good time and fun in cosy surroundings. The concept of *hygge* is fundamental to the comfortable home and translates, in decor terms, into: a dominant fireplace and a comfy spot in all corners.

02
Natural material, colour and texture. The use of natural materials is prevalent in a comfortable home. In this living room the palette includes a shiny copper chimney at the end of which is a patinated copper fireplace, a handmade brick hearth, unfinished, hand-turned timber furniture, leather, brushed-cotton and wool soft furnishings, and an animal-skin rug.

03
Upholstery. Both seat and scatter cushions need to be inviting, enveloping and deeply comfortable. In this living room the promise of cosiness is reiterated in the availability of a knitted throw.

04
Wear and care. The comfortable home is the naturally evolving home: the leather cushions on this sofa will soften and improve with age; the aesthetics of the copper and brick fireplace will develop their appeal with use; the timber furniture will attract a familiar narrative of inevitable scratches as time goes by.

comfortable

01
This dining space is comfortably informal: surplus crockery is decoratively mounted on top of the cabinet, and a candelabra and other charming accessories jostle for position above the raw brick fireplace. The look is completed with a farmhouse table, mismatched chairs and seat cushions all in a neutral colour palette.

02
An inviting and cosy room, perfectly illustrating the comfortable look. All that's required here is a box of chocolates and a good book.

03
The scrubbed table, comfy seating, kitchen stove and neutral palette all play their part here to create a comfortable room scheme.

02

03

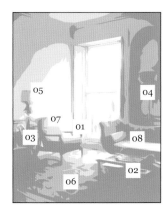

eclectic

The term 'eclectic' is often confused with what is simply a mishmash, a cover-all term for unfocused decorating. To create a convincing and, moreover, satisfying eclectic 'look' there is one simple rule: while the components may be diverse – from mixed historical periods to a mix of materials – one or more characteristics of each component must be echoed at least once in another. Components include wall and floor finishes and doors and windows as well as furniture, lighting and accessories. The characteristics fall into four categories: colour, material, shape and texture.

Once you have identified the individual characteristics, no matter how multifaceted – for example, circular and geometric shapes, tubular metal, a white/blue/dark brown colour palette, mid-toned wood, organic features – any components you add that comply in at least one respect with your framework will 'work'.

The ability to create satisfying eclectic design schemes is worth mastering, as it is perhaps the most 'natural' style of home decor. Our homes are, after all, a kind of gallery of the self and will inevitably attract a multitude of meaningful objects over the years, objects that will be best appreciated when thoughtfully curated.

key ingredients

Colour scheme. Colours in an eclectic decorative scheme can be whatever you choose, but you must be disciplined. Here the palette is green, gold, silver and caramel, and each component features at least one of these colours.

Material palette. The same discipline applies to materials. Here the material palette consists principally of timber, metal, glass and silk. The contemporary chair frames (01) relate to the 1970's table frame (02); the silver metal and reflectivity in the Deco side table (03) compares to that in the 1970's Guzzini floor lamp (04), and the mirrored glass table top (03) to that of the central table (02) as well as the crystal drops in the 1930's side lamp (05). The green and gold lurex-flecked rug (06) picks out the gold in that same lamp (05) and echoes the pale green of the walls and armchair upholstery (07). The gold silk Victorian chaise (08) relates to the gold silk lamp shade and gilt lamp base.

Shape. There is also the shared element of shape to consider. Here curves are represented in the floor lamp (04), the chaise (08) and the silk lamp shade (05). There are even radii to be spotted in the chair and table frames (01, 02 and 03).

eclectic

01

While some of the furnishings here are decidedly retro, it is the number of contemporary pieces stirred into the mix, such as the bed, side lamp, chest of drawers and picture collection, that puts this scheme on the eclectic side of the fence, all held together with a consistent colour palette. Note how the mirrored wall sculpture echoes the arrangement of pictures on the adjacent wall.

02

A very architectural environment is spiced up with a mix consisting of a Campana Brothers armchair upholstered with soft toys, a traditional crystal chandelier and gilded Thonet dining chair. It is the clever use of off-white, gold and caramel colours that make the whole scheme hang together.

03

Burnt orange, peacock blue and white is always an appealing colour combination and here three colours are splashed over a diverse but harmonious collection of furnishings and fittings.

handcrafted

Simple, everyday objects that feature the poetic imperfections of the handmade take centre stage in the handcrafted look, which is freestanding and loose fitting.

Everything from stools and cooking utensils to tablecloths and mortars are selected not only to fulfil a function but for their naive artistic quality, too – a quality that also expresses the narrative of making; the processes employed and the labour expended.

To highlight these characteristics walls, floors, doors and windows are necessarily recessive and simple, too – chalky, matt paints and basic structure suffices.

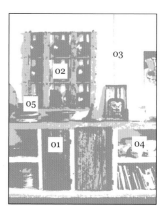

key ingredients

01
Resourcefulness. Beautifully worn reclaimed timber planks are reinvented as cabinet doors and an old wooden pallet becomes plate rack.

02
Artisanship and the irresistibility of touch. Hand-thrown, and therefore unique, plates, bowls and pots add sculptural character to this kitchen.

03
Quiet colour. Colours are quiet and recessive, as in the whitewash on the walls of this kitchen, or dark and earthy, as in its contents.

04
Intimacy. Small- to medium-scale spaces are well disposed to handcrafted homes, where the detail in carefully selected objects can be fully and frequently appreciated.

05
Natural materials. Readily available natural materials are a welcome inevitability, though any material, natural or man-made, that is recycled by hand has a place in the handcrafted home.

handcrafted

01
Bamboo furniture, raw plaster walls, hand-woven textiles and rough wooden shutters create a charming sleeping space.

02
Hand-thrown pots, scrubbed timber and exotic sculptures are highlighted against a fresh, white background and complemented by a rough slate floor.

03
A sculpted cave-like interior offers visceral comfort. The organic white space is enlivened by attention-grabbing hand-woven textiles and objects nestling in seamless recesses. There is also a pleasing contrast between the smoothness of the walls and the roughness of the door.

handcrafted

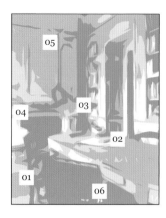

historical

By 'historical' home I am not referring to any particular period, or precise restoration thereof, but something more abstract and so more open to romantic interpretation.

The simple fact is there is comfort to be found in aged surroundings, where familiarity combines with the promise of the time continuum and tactile patinas. This is why the ersatz of reproduction is so popular, in both architecture and furnishings.

But the success of the historical home is wholly dependent on the genuine. This means the use of, at best, reclaimed and, at the least, natural materials – and real antique furniture, accessories and even hardware. When the genuine is not available, then reproduction is the only option but reproduction will, generally speaking, be convincing only if the materials or crafts employed are of historical record.

Where the modern day intrudes – for example, in light switches – these features need not chime figuratively with the overall scheme, as it will be clear they are fake, as in 'Georgian-style' brass light switches with twisted 'Adam-style' rope detailing. Instead, new fittings should echo the sensuality of age: colour, texture and density can all contribute to that kind of satisfying weightiness that is a consistent feature of 'historical' objects. And new interventions like these – and this is crucial – should be extremely simple and recessive. Indeed, simplicity and restraint are fundamental to success here, to allow the cherished imperfections of aged finishes and objects the space to resonate.

key ingredients

01
Antiques (or good reproductions). Each piece of furniture in this 18th-century space may not be from that period but is antique, and bears the distinctive form, finishes and even wear and tear of such.

02
Natural materials. Nothing but natural, as opposed to synthetic, materials are persuasive in historical homes.

03
Restraint. The structure of rooms in a historical home often constitute the main appeal, so any objects introduced into the space must be of a character and quantity that allows walls and floors to be enjoyed as much as the items themselves.

04
Atmospheric lighting. Crepuscular illumination is a characteristic of historical homes: candle light, oil lamps, incandescent bulbs – these all serve to create the requisite historical atmosphere.

05
Aged surfaces. The wash on the panelling in this dining room, and the scrubbed table, speak of use and the poetic passage of time, all essential to the historical home.

06
Formality. Here the idea of formality is defined by symmetry and quality materials.

historical

01
Aged surfaces are taken to the extreme here, where paint is allowed to decoratively peel. An antique wardrobe, chair and richly embroidered bed covering complete the scene.

02
Quietly beautiful furniture, combined with a simple window dressing and a colour scheme redolent of the more daring tendencies of the 18th century constitute this historical drawing room.

03
The white detail on a pair of Wedgwood green vitrines is echoed in the carefully organized contents and the striking, traditional black and white checked floor, complete with fine antique table and chair.

04
Perfect symmetry, soft true-to-period green walls, candles and a table laid with antique cutlery (flatware) and glassware complement the original Georgian fireplace and adjacent joinery to create a well-mannered but no less inviting atmosphere.

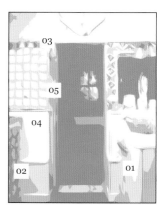

retro

Entering a retro home should be like discovering a childhood scrapbook, full of memory and playfulness, all viewed with a fresh perspective. 'Retro' is derived from the Latin prefix *retro*, meaning 'moving backward' or of 'past times'. But retro's rearward glance is not infinite; its field of vision is firmly bounded by the cultural recovery of the post-war 1950s and principally embraces the styles of not only the 1950s but the 1960s and 1970s, too. In retro we can benefit from the comforting nostalgia of a previous period while being energized by post-war optimism.

To achieve a pleasing retro look, the heroes of the day are genuine retro furnishings. You can either echo their characteristics in wall and floor finishes or contrast them against more neutral backgrounds.

key ingredients

01
Real retro. Genuine retro features, from the patterned sticky-backed plastic on the cupboards and walls to the beverage canisters and even the refrigerator and sink, mark this kitchen out as unambiguously retro.

02
Retro-style environment. Note also how other wall finishes and decorative elements are convincingly retro, from the tongue-and-groove panelling to the rugs. Another way of describing this feature is simply 'retro texture'.

03
Display. Retro is theatrical, where we play at living in another time and place, and display is an essential form of this kind of expression, represented here by a row of jars carefully mounted, label outward, on top of a cupboard; the vertical row of jugs, and the blue plastic fruit basket.

04
Colour. Pastel pink complements the fittings and finishes here, and exaggerates the retro feel.

05
Playfulness. Pink is most certainly a playful colour and this, combined with the displays, indicates the owners are enjoying themselves here.

retro

01
An otherwise neutral space is energized with retro furniture and upholstery.

03
The tessellated wall treatment, more shagpile carpet and the 1950's furniture scream brat pack… and retro.

02
Shagpile carpeting, the classic Eero Aarnio suspended Bubble Chair and 1970's ceiling light are complemented by retro flourishes, such as the full gathered curtains set behind an integrated pelmet and a reflective, textured ceiling.

04
A mix of retro furniture, upholstery and accessories clarify a retro colour scheme.

4
space for everything

4

space for everything

In his 1974 essay 'Species of Spaces' the provocative French author Georges Perec ruminates on the way our homes are divided and our living spaces classified. He observes how the functions of the broom cupboard and the bedroom are one and the same: 'recuperation and maintenance'.

As an alternative, Perec proposes the idea of dividing spaces in terms of senses – 'a smellery' or 'an auditory' – and even 'heptadian' ('hepta' as in seven, 'adian' as in circadian) rhythms, where each day of the week corresponds to a different space in a home. On Mondays, for example, life would be lived solely in the 'Mondayery'. Perec goes on to develop this idea by theming his concept of 'daily rooms', inspired by a Paris brothel – which is where his themes should firmly remain.

Rethinking our approach to the way we organize the space we inhabit shifts control over the way we live our lives,

transferring it from the often anonymous architects, or even the previous occupants, who laid out our homes, to us, who live in them now. The philosopher Henri Bergson alludes to this idea when he writes, 'The objects which surround my body reflect its possible action upon them.' The locations of interactive objects in a space, rather than the space itself, are the primary force in determining the function of the space. For example, where a bath is located in a bedroom, the conventional descriptions of 'bathroom' and 'bedroom' are no longer relevant, nor restrictive.

bathing

Over recent years the bathroom has been contrived as a 'home spa', a place of refuge and relaxation, as well as somewhere to brush your teeth. Bathing has been liberated from the shackles of dreary utility to realize its potential for pleasure. This places even greater demands on the design process, because the places where we bathe – which are usually confined areas – are now expected to be dream spaces as well as highly practical and hardworking.

01
A fantasy shower room made real, where the feel of a crisp country morning on hot, wet skin makes for an unbeatable start to the day.

02
This bathroom is sufficiently spacious to incorporate a handy chair, and the combination of a molasses-coloured timber finish behind the sink and fresh white walls and floors makes for a good balance between fresh and warming.

LAYOUT

To tackle the challenge, first think about what kind of functions will be required. Just as you asked yourself questions to set out your design brief (page 14), now is the time to get into detail with the following questions:

- Do I want a shower as well as a bath?
- If so, would I prefer the shower to be separate from the bath?
- If a separate shower, do I want a shower tray or a tiled floor, wet-room style?
- What kind of toiletries or accessories do I want to store in the shower?
- Would I like a panelled or freestanding bathtub?
- What kind of toiletries or accessories would I like to store close to the bath?
- Do I want to incorporate a toilet?
- If so, where do I want to store spare toilet paper and accessories?
- Do I want to incorporate a bidet?
- One sink or two?
- What style of sink(s) do I want (such as pedestal style, inset into a vanity unit or a bowl type sitting on top of it)?
- How many toiletries do I need to accommodate in total?
- Do I want to accommodate cleaning materials, too?
- Where will I store towels?
- Where will I dispose of towels ready for laundering?
- What kind of towel rail do I want – one that is heated all year round or one that just comes on with the central heating?
- Will I need to accommodate an electric shaver or toothbrush?
- Do I need to store children's bath toys?
- Do I need to accommodate infirmities?

You will then need to match requirements to the space available and even the strength of your floor. An extra-large or cast-iron bath full of water may just be too heavy for the floor to cope without strengthening it.

Bear in mind that you do not need to centralize all these needs in a single space – in fact, separating out functions can be helpful. For example, a separate toilet will always take the strain off the main bathroom in a large household. Depending on where it is sited, it may also mean that guests can use it and do not need to intrude on private space.

In the same vein you could consider locating your bath or shower in your bedroom, though you will need to pay attention to your local building regulations. Water and electricity, as in bedside lamps, are not the best mix, and ventilation is an important factor.

An outdoor shower may seem crazy in cooler climes, but if privacy, as well as proximity to a dressing area, can be guaranteed, a hot shower outdoors, on even the most brisk of days, is delicious and also very handy. However, distributing bathroom plumbing around your home to accommodate this will obviously cost more.

Recommended dimensions

The standard dimensions of sanitaryware –
baths, showers, toilets, bidets, sinks – and
their recommended clearances are as follows:

	Standard depth/size	Clearance to front	Clearance to side
Bath	1700 x 700mm (67 x 27½in)	n/a	700mm (27½in)
Shower	900 x 900mm (35½ x 35½in)	700mm (27½in)	n/a
Sink	400mm (15¾in)	700mm (27½in)	200mm (8in)
Toilet	700mm (27½in)	600mm (24in)	200mm (8in)
Bidet	700mm (27½in)	600mm (24in)	300mm (12in)

These are just standards, however.
Freestanding baths generally take up
more space than panelled baths and
all sanitaryware comes in many sizes.
Clearances can also be adjusted according
to preference, though personal experience
has taught me that it can be useful to
measure users when drawing up a layout.

If you are trying to squeeze in a smaller
than standard shower, bear in mind that the
width and depth need to equate to the widest
shoulder breadth plus at least 400mm
(16in). The most effective weapon in the
battle for good design is the tape measure.

Height is another factor to consider.
Sanitaryware such as sinks and showers

01

The bedroom in this loft apartment serves as bathroom, too, where a consistent colour palette reinforces the integration of two, usually separate, functions.

02

The designer of this bathroom has evidently thought very carefully about storage, creating generous capacity that elegantly fits around the sanitaryware.

02

will obviously require full height clearance. Baths, toilets and bidets can be squeezed into areas with less height, if necessary.

Siting and sighting

Plumbing requirements will affect the layout of your bathroom, meaning that you won't have a completely free hand.

☐ If you are refurbishing, note that while you might be replacing sanitaryware, it will be less expensive to retain the same type in the same location.

☐ If you are incorporating a toilet (with or without a bidet) in the bathroom, try to avoid it being the first thing you see as

you enter. Perhaps you could hide it behind a screen or a short wall. Your bathroom will feel just a bit more luxurious and less utilitarian as a result.

☐ Unless you install a macerator (a rather noisy machine that propels waste from a toilet to a distant soil pipe), locate the toilet adjacent to the soil pipe.

Brassware

When selecting brassware – taps (faucets), shower heads, wastes, thermostatic shower controls, hand showers – check that it is compatible with your sanitaryware. Pay specific attention to the 'throw' of taps, which the depth of your sink will need to

accommodate comfortably. For more about choosing brassware, see page 202.

When positioning shower controls, try to locate them out of the fall of water from the shower head above. This way you can avoid getting drenched before you are ready.

The purist in me has done away with a hand shower in a shower stall or adjacent to a bath, at least in my own homes. If you are similarly inclined, resist the temptation. A bath or shower without a hand shower will be a devil to clean, and you will not be able to wash your hair satisfactorily in the bath, either. The most discreet hand showers are what are called 'microphone' showers. These can be recessed into a bath surround.

LIFE'S LUXURIES

In the spirit of the home spa, you may like to consider installing the following 'luxury' features:

The big stuff

☐ A steam shower, the classy alternative to the Jacuzzi bath, complete with a little seat. It is surprisingly easy and relatively affordable to convert standard showers into more sumptuous steam versions.

☐ A Jacuzzi bath, if you don't mind bathing in what usually sounds like a waste-disposal unit macerating a teaspoon, no matter how high quality.

☐ An extra-large shower for two, with two shower heads. Likewise an extra-large bath for two, or two baths side by side.

☐ A sauna – very 1970s but still quite sexy, though very space-hungry.

☐ An overflow or infinity bath, which allows you to fill the bath to the brim and then sink in up to your neck, the overflow being captured by a secondary 'bath' or skin. This option is not particularly water-efficient, however.

The little stuff

☐ Books – there's nothing like reading in the bath. Or sketching. A special book rest for a bath helps.

☐ Candles and incense, of course – but consider designing in special recesses for them.

☐ Flowers and plants – most love moist environments.

☐ Music and entertainment, from either a bathroom radio or a humidity-resistant overhead speaker. You could also have a waterproof bathroom television, if you must.

☐ Art, in two or three dimensions (but make sure it won't be affected by the steam).

01

01
The generous proportions of this bathroom have been capitalized on to create a two-person walk-in shower, complete with a smart frameless screen.

02
Bathroom becomes 'spa room' with a luxurious infinity bath and cute bamboo tray of bathing accessories.

03
The loose-fitting, artistic style of this bathroom creates a romantic atmosphere for bathing.

01

A long, thin space creates a dynamic bathing 'line', where shower, toilet and sink sit along one wall with full-height storage opposite.

02

Here, the bath and shower have been constructed using identical elements: tiled concrete form. In doing so, the owner is liberated from the standard sizes of ready-made sanitaryware, making this a good solution where space is limited.

02

SPACE-SAVING

If you cannot accommodate everything you want to, you will need to prioritize or streamline your requirements. Wet rooms are extremely space-efficient, making the most out of the space available. Systems have developed significantly so that even timber-framed floors can have a wet room fitted over the top without the risk of leak-causing cracks.

To prevent water from spilling out of the bathroom – in the event of a blocked drain, say – be sure to install a threshold strip approximately 5mm ($^1/_4$in) higher than the rest of the floor. Note that the depth of your joists will determine the finished floor level (FFL). The shallower the joists, the more limited the gradient (the 'fall') over which water can drain away, in which case it may be necessary to raise the floor to achieve effective drainage. This in turn may require a step up into the wet room, which is not always desirable.

It is possible to buy compact sanitaryware, such as Japanese-style bathtubs, where luxurious depth compensates for the shortness. Entire ranges of sanitaryware are designed for restricted spaces, from corner baths and toilets to shallow hand-wash sinks that can be partly recessed into the wall.

In bathrooms that are small in floor space but have high ceilings, modulating the floor level is the key to fitting in all you want. I once saw a bathroom in which a sunken bath was fitted with a cover that could be walked on in order to use a sink above.

Sliding doors are very space-efficient. I have designed tiny, jewel-like en suite bathrooms incorporating these. Where there is no window in the bathroom, I fit the sliding door with a panel of two-way mirror glass, allowing for light to penetrate while the mirroring effect protects privacy.

TEAR-FREE FAMILY BATHING TIPS

☐ Two sinks are often installed in a bathroom so that more than one person can use the bathroom at once, but an alternative is to install a large sink with two sets of taps (faucets).

☐ In a household with teenagers, the boarding house standby of installing sinks in their bedrooms can be an excellent way of relieving pressure

on the family bathroom. A neat way of doing this is to conceal the sink behind a cupboard door.

☐ Small children will not be able to reach standard-height sinks and toilets. In this case you could install wall-hung versions adjusted to their diminutive height. But children do grow, so a more flexible alternative is to provide a mobile step.

WALLS AND FLOORS

The presence of water demands waterproof surfaces that will not fail when wet, protecting the environment and users alike. Hard, hermetic, 'wipe dry' materials are the most appropriate and range from specialist paint to ceramic tile, and from stone to sheets of composite.

Wallpaper in areas of the bathroom that are not in direct contact with water is feasible, so long as there is sufficient ventilation and the wallpaper has been applied well, but there is obviously some risk of failure as paper is porous. Vinyl wallpapers are the usual choice in bathing areas, but there are environmental issues to consider in the manufacture and use of vinyl products (see Chapter 5, page 162).

Water not only can damage floor finishes, especially if left standing – carpet and wood-laminate flooring are but two examples of materials that actively absorb water – but can also harm the bather. While regulations usually dictate the use of nonslip flooring in public spaces, this rule does not apply to private homes. Nevertheless, there is wisdom in ensuring that floor surfaces in bathing areas provide sufficient purchase. Slip-resistant flooring suitable for use in bathrooms or wet rooms include ceramic or stone tiles with a textured surface, or small tiles, in which the close spacing of grout lines fulfils the same purpose.

01
The mix of a reflective, black rubber floor and glossy white surfaces is focused in a single element of black-and-white 'optical' laminate facing the vanity unit.

02
Small, white, hexagonal tiles on walls and floors provide a nonslip surface underfoot and offer a unifying surface finish.

03
Painted brick combined with smooth terrazzo and timber floor finishes, and a shiny white bath, creates a seductive palette of rough and smooth, matte and gloss.

LIGHTING

Good overhead lighting is essential, but the best for makeup is side lighting. To modulate the ambience, put overhead lights on a dimmer switch or install a separate ambient-lighting circuit. LEDs (light-emitting diodes) are energy-efficient and tiny, and the best-quality models can create dramatic effects. Note that any light fixtures you use in your bathroom will need to be designed specifically for bathrooms in order to comply with safety regulations.

01

02

03

WINDOWS

To alleviate any sense of claustrophobia in a windowless bathroom, the sense of a window can be suggested using a light box. Do this by fitting a recess in a wall or ceiling with an artificial light fitting – a fluorescent tube inside a blue gel works very well – and cover it with opaque glass or Perspex (Plexiglas).

If there is no window, you will need ventilation. Regulations in some countries demand that this is wired into the main lighting circuit, with a delayed 'time out' – where the fan will run for a short while after you have left the bathroom and turned out the light. Personally I cannot bear the sound of these noisy things while I am using a bathroom and usually have them wired in such a way that they can be turned on and off at will.

If a bathroom does feature a window, try to orientate the bath and shower toward any particularly lovely (and private) view. Bathing in these circumstances will always feel gloriously sensual, even on grey days.

Steam dictates that bathroom window dressings be kept minimal – a simple shade, for example. You could even dispense with the window dressing entirely and instead replace the clear glass with acid-etched glass, which allows the maximum ingress of daylight as well as privacy. A less expensive alternative is semi-opaque window film, but do have a professional glazier apply it: bubbles should be kept to the bath.

MIRRORS

A heated mirror will not steam up. And an illuminated magnifying mirror is illuminating, though the reflection may occasionally be alarming.

If the sink is located beneath a window, just suspend the mirror above it from ceiling fixings, or choose a mirror that can be hinged at one side of the window. The former will make for excellent makeup light, since you will receive daylight from both sides, at least in the daytime.

In most bathrooms, the sink requires both a splashback and a mirror. A more streamlined solution is to combine the two, in the form of a splashback made of mirror.

The ample use of mirrors and glass is tempting in what is often a small space, but remember, shiny surfaces need to be kept shiny, or your bathroom will just look grubby. There is also the small matter of multiple reflections of your naked or semi-clothed self, which may or may not be welcome.

The density of a milk chocolate colour scheme is levitated by a dynamic tile shape and a collection of wall-mounted elements, from the toilet to the vanity surface and mirrored cabinets. Shaver sockets (outlets) are hidden within the cabinets while glass shelves above the concealed cistern satisfy less utilitarian demands.

02

An unusually shaped space is given an unusual treatment, where elements are as imaginative as they are useful.

03

In this bedroom/bathroom suite concrete has been used to mould the sink and shower to exact specifications; the mirror performs as a reflector and splashback, and the lavish shower curtain shares the same qualities as the window dressings in the adjacent bedroom, softening the hard edges.

Heating

Underfloor heating is ideal in a bathroom, as this is the most effective way of drying water splashes on the floor. It is rare, though, that such a system will supply sufficient heat for the entire room, in which case a radiator may also be required, depending on the output of any heated towel rail (towel warmer). When drawing up your plan, do allow for wall space for a radiator.

Towels

The only way to effectively dry wet or damp towels in a limited space is with a heated towel rail that can be heated independently of your central-heating system. In general, more flexibility will equate to more cost. Make sure that towels are within easy reach of a shower or bath, and remember to allow for wall space for your towel rail when drawing up your plan.

You may need to store clean spare towels somewhere, too, perhaps in built-in or freestanding cabinets or shelves, or on wall-mounted towel racks that hold folded clean towels on top. If you have room, it is useful to install a laundry basket to hold used towels. Some bathrooms incorporate a laundry chute so that used bathroom towels can be sent to the laundry room below, but it is important that children cannot gain access, as the temptation of an in-house joyride can be irresistible.

Electricity

The best place to locate sockets (outlets) for electric toothbrushes and shavers is inside a bathroom cabinet, where devices can be recharged and detached for use. There is hardly need for display. In many countries, only shaver sockets with transformers are safe (and legal) to be installed in bathrooms, and regular electrical sockets may not be allowed at all, so be sure to comply with your country's building regulations.

Storage

In any bathroom, cleaning materials and medicines, as well as uglier toiletries, should be stored out of sight and out of reach of small children for reasons of both aesthetics and safety. A mirrored cabinet with adjustable shelves is a common solution, being dual-function. It is worth measuring what you need to store to ensure your cabinet is big enough.

For toiletries that you wish to keep close to hand, a recess adjacent to the bath or inside the shower will work well. The base should have an almost imperceptible incline so that water can drain away. A recess with a mirrored back can create a sense of depth.

If you have small children, you will need to store bath toys somewhere. A box with a padded lid, perhaps upholstered in bathroom-style fabric such as terry towelling, will not only offer storage but also allow you to take a seat while keeping an eye on the children. If space is tight, a net bag fixed to the wall will keep toys tidy after bath time.

Accessories

Often when I walk into a beautiful bathroom I am surprised at how clear it is that no one thought about where to put waste. I realize it is not the most attractive subject, but this is why it needs extra thought. If you are installing any built-ins, you may want to consider a recessed bin. This solution will also relieve floor space. Any kind of attractive vessel with a lid would also work well. And while recycling kitchen waste is practically standard, this is not the case with bathroom waste, though there is no reason why the same principles should not apply.

Given that space is usually limited in a bathroom, it will be worthwhile thinking when drawing up your plan about where you will locate other accessories, such as a toilet brush, toilet-paper holder, tissue box, toothbrush holder, glasses and any cachepots for cotton balls, cotton buds (Q-tips) and the like. Wall-mounting them or placing them on small wall-mounted shelves will relieve floor and counter space.

Convenience and safety

If you are installing any fixture with integrated working parts, such as an integrated bath, or a wall-hung toilet or sink, be sure also to fit an access panel so that parts can be easily repaired or, more likely, unblocked.

As mentioned under Storage, if small children have access to a bathroom, it is essential that medicines, cleaning fluids, toiletries and sharp implements be stored in out-of-reach cupboards behind doors fitted with safety latches. In the same vein, make sure that any door locks are fitted out of the reach of children, high up, so that they do not imprison themselves.

If the elderly and infirm are using the bathroom, there needs to be sufficient and appropriately located grab bars and seating, as necessary – for example, in a shower or beside a bath – and all floor surfaces must be slip-resistant. A bathroom designed for those who are physically impaired does not need to look like something out of a hospital: it just needs a bit more thought to ensure that beauty is matched by practicality, which is the basis of all good design.

cleaning

Cleaning a home and its contents is a necessary chore. But accommodating bulky housekeeping tools – brooms, ironing boards, vacuum cleaners, buckets – and even the not-so-bulky, such as dust cloths and cleaning fluids, need not be a chore, so long as careful consideration is given to where and how these might best be stored, so that they do not intrude on the rest of your home.

02

01
A washing machine and dryer are neatly tucked away in a shower room.

02
Traditionally made cleaning equipment is as good to look at as it is effective.

A utility room is ideal, even it is very small. The full height of the room should ideally be used and abused. I have buckets and baskets hanging from the walls and ceiling in my own, plus lots of shelving and recycling bins.

In a tight squeeze a radical alternative is to display the bulkier cleaning tools, such as brushes and vacuum cleaners, but you can really only get away with this if the objects themselves have some appealing quality beyond basic utility. This is not such a preposterous idea: the all-white vacuum cleaner by the Swedish designer Pia Wallén for Electrolux is as seductive as any other well-designed object, while some of the most beautiful things are the most simple.

I always find old-fashioned brushes, made out of natural materials, charming. The potential of this concept has been gloriously realized by the German designers Oliver Vogt and Hermann Weizenegger of V+W, who worked with the German Blind Institute and several other talented product designers to create a collection of exquisite brushes.

Laundry
Washing machines and dryers are commonly sited in a kitchen or adjacent utility room, but there is some merit in locating a dedicated laundry room adjacent to bedrooms instead, since this is where most laundry is generated. Ultimately, though, it is simply a matter of personal preference. For those who like to hang their laundry outside to dry, the passage from washing machine inside to drying line outside may be a consideration. Likewise, the sound of a vibrating washing machine penetrating bedrooms may not be welcome. Another option is to create a dedicated space where laundry can be discreetly hung to dry inside.

connecting

Inside any home there are spaces that only connect: stairwells, landings, corridors, passageways. These connections can be called 'transitional spaces' – areas that transport you from one room to the next. Another kind of transitional space is a threshold, where the interior of a home connects to the exterior via doors, windows, entry hall, porch, mudroom, terrace, garden, pathways, driveway, conservatory or sunroom.

Providing a sense of place, privacy, protection and invitation, as well as connection, are the various roles of transitional spaces. Because these abstract and sometimes contradictory concepts are difficult to grasp, it can be tempting to remove a transitional space without thought for the implications.

For example, I have visited many homes where the entry hall has been incorporated into the adjacent living room to make the living room larger – it does, but not without loss of privacy. Suddenly the living room is the entry hall, and a visitor's gaze can penetrate a great deal of private space without necessarily being invited to do so.

I also remember seeing a home by a celebrated architect in which the corridor to the side of the bedrooms had been done away with to make the bedrooms larger. People were expected to walk to the bathroom at the end of the building through others' bedrooms.

Similarly, I find it depressing to see front gardens concreted over to create parking space. Gardens not only stitch a building into its landscape but, in the midst of brick and concrete, are an important reminder of our place in the natural world. Which is why, in the absence of a garden, well-tended house plants and window boxes can help to energize a home.

01

The sometimes abstract concept of connection in a home is made crystal clear here, where the house's facade photographically duplicates its environs.

Intense lemon yellow is served
up as a momentary, invigorating
splash in this hotel hallway.

ENTRY HALLS AND CORRIDORS

The effectiveness of entry halls and corridors can be informed by shape. Just as a friendly arm around your back can guide you to a particular destination, so a curving wall or a floor decal can guide you to a particular doorway.

Because these spaces are experienced momentarily, there is also opportunity for the kind of dramatization that might be too wearing in spaces where you spend more time. Highly decorative surfaces and whimsical objects can stimulate and amuse in satisfyingly small bites.

In terms of practicalities, entry halls should be unobstructed and hardwearing.

Wall surfaces should be fairly tough, and flooring will need to be able to cope with passing traffic and be easily cleaned of outdoor grit, too. If shoes are expected to be removed near the front door, it can be helpful to install some kind of seat and neat shoe storage.

Good lighting is important, striking a balance between being functional – so you can see where you are and where you are going – and atmospheric. Decorative pendant lighting is an effective solution. Recessed wall lights, mounted just a little way up a wall, will illuminate any changes in floor level.

01

02
This hallway also operates as a gallery and storage area, where large-format images of the household's children are laminated onto sliding and concealing panels. Each child can identify their space from their own picture.

03
Traditional Victorian encaustic floor tiles have been laid not only on the floors of this Victorian hallway, but on the wall, too, creating an indestructible wall surface in a heavy-traffic area of the home, and a provocative challenge to convention.

04
Gilt walls and decorative floor tiles offer a hit of glamour as well as a hardwearing surface.

You may also need somewhere to put the mail and keys. A slim console table or a shelf can be suitable, but beware of exposing important items, as these can be easily filched by bad people with long sticks poked through your letterbox. A small cupboard may be better.

Any other objects, such as coats, shoes, hats and umbrellas, should be neatly stored away, too, though not necessarily out of sight. The objective here is not purity but minimizing chaos and clumsy obstructions. If you are considering hooks, look out for sculptural designs to add subtle character to a space with few requisite features.

Thresholds are generally draughty places, so both heating and insulation will be helpful. Something as basic as a double-lined curtain, mounted behind the front door, and a stuffed 'sausage-dog' will help to exclude draughts, but you should also inspect the seals in doors and windows to ensure they are effective. In small entry halls, a recessed radiator or underfloor heating is the most space-friendly heating solution.

The uninterrupted expanse of wall in corridors and passageways creates instant gallery space, where pictures can be carefully illuminated by picture lights or directional ceiling lights. A mirror can make a small entry hall feel larger, and ensure you do not leave the house looking any different to how you would want to be seen.

03

04

01

A traditional hallway is given a non-traditional treatment: cornicing is picked out in dark grey on white and an antique chandelier is mixed up with contemporarily contrasting and amusing accessories, where a well chosen set of coat hooks speaks volumes.

02

Here, the melting point between upper and lower floors exists at the white-as-white wall behind the open-tread, minimally balustered staircase.

03

Sticky-backed plastic in a graphic print applied to the stair risers brightens this hallway.

MUDROOMS

A 'mudroom' at the rear of a home, even if it is little more than a porch or vestibule, will help to protect the interior from muddy boots, and paws. Pet paraphernalia and any other outdoor equipment can be stored here.

STAIRWELLS

Open treads or glass treads on a stairway help to distribute light between upstairs and downstairs. Balustrades and handrails are sometimes removed for the same reason, but there are safety issues involved here and building regulations can sometimes circumscribe what you can and cannot do.

Traditional timber stairs will always be much more quiet if carpeted, and a stair runner can look particularly elegant. In one home that I designed, to make an ugly banister look more fetching without spending a great deal of money, I had the handrail painted in the same olive green as the stair runner. In this way, the handrail played a supporting role in the striking effect of the carpet, instead of compromising it.

01
1960s-style, segmented and frosted-glass panels makes this window just that bit more interesting, inside and out.

02
Tutti-frutti-coloured glass panels in these double doors provide privacy, coloured light and decorative appeal.

03
An aged, studded timber door opens onto a newly cobbled floor surface and smooth, dark honey coloured timber panelling to create a concert of touch-me textures. I wonder how many times that door has opened? And onto what? And whom?

WINDOWS AND DOORS

The style of the windows and doors in a home will have enormous impact on its look and feel. The size of a window will influence daylight penetration, but the window frames can have immense aesthetic influence. In particular, the finish, proportions and detail of white, plastic-framed replacement windows do not complement historic buildings. Nor is it possible to paint or repair them, unlike timber or metal frames. Once white plastic is installed, you are stuck with it, until it yellows and deteriorates and needs to be disposed of (and is unlikely to be recyclable).

Sadly, plastic is prevalent in many front doors, too, which may also feature fake leaded and stained-glass panels. These are hideous. Doors need to feel weighty and solid, protective and reassuring, and front doors need to be inviting, too, deftly incorporating opposite impressions. Your choice of material, colour, hardware and adjacent lighting will help to strike the balance. Toughened-glass panels will help to increase the amount of daylight inside.

The desert of Palm Springs
becomes part of the furniture in
this home designed by Marmol
Radziner, where the use of large
windows and dusty colours bring
the outside inside.

02

A church spire is perfectly and
deliberately framed by the window
in this David Adjaye-designed
London home.

02

BORROWED LANDSCAPE

If you are lucky enough to live amid impressive views, such a blessing can be amplified by the clever shaping of a window, or adjusting the shape of an existing window, to the landscape. For example, in a London house designed by the architect David Adjaye a well-placed vertical window deliberately captures the view of a pretty church spire.

This device is known as 'borrowed landscape', in which elements outside a boundary are incorporated in some way within that boundary, by either repetition or simple acknowledgment, as in the case of the Adjaye house. Commonly used in landscape design during the 18th century, it serves the same purpose today – to connect and extend a space by drawing the eye to a distant view.

DISSOLVING THRESHOLDS

Thresholds can be further 'dissolved' by minimizing any obstruction between inside and out. I have designed many homes where I have had full-height and full-width glass doors fitted, but have then also made sure that the same flooring material – usually stone but porcelain tile is a good alternative – is used inside and out. In this way the inside space will feel larger than it is, and because the number of elements is restrained, the whole is inescapably elegant.

If you are using wooden floorboards inside, you could create a similar effect by using the same width of decking boards outside. Just be sure to run the boards in the same direction. (Boards running front to back instead of side to side will lengthen the sense of perspective.)

01

In this London home the patio is paved in the same material and at the same height as the adjacent kitchen. Sliding glass doors retract to meld inside space with outside. The use of bright yellow and coral colours in both zones reinforces this happy marriage.

02

Large glass doors play their part in dissolving the threshold between a bathroom and its courtyard, where the pool outside is resonant of the bath inside, and vice versa, heightening the sensual aspects of the bathing experience.

03

A perimeter wall retracts fully in this home, welcoming in the rainforest beyond. Inside, tribute is paid to the forest's fecundity in the form of a tropical fruit-shaped pendant light fitting.

cooking

An abiding cliché is that the kitchen is the heart of the home. And as households become more fragmented – with more people living alone, more single-parent families, fewer elders living with their adult children and declining birth rates – it is notable just how much more tempting new kitchen designs have become. It is as if we are compensating for the decline in Waltons-style family fantasy.

Perhaps this is too cynical a note on which to begin a section on the subject of cooking, which can be one of the most creative and loving activities we perform. But it is a phenomenon worth acknowledging, if only to guard against being distracted by fancy toys and so lose sight of what we really need. And like.

It is a fact, though, that 'tools do not a chef make'. Elizabeth David, the celebrated 20th-century cookery writer, cooked for most of her life in a very basic kitchen consisting of a four-ring gas stove, a Welsh dresser (hutch) and a large wooden kitchen table. In those days dining rooms were the norm, so there was not as much pressure on the kitchen to look seductive as there is now, when many kitchens are open-plan to dining spaces. Nevertheless, the point on 'tools' is instructive.

The celebrity chef Gary Rhodes once cooked in my London loft apartment for a photo shoot, and I will never forget his crushing comment as he arrived – 'I've got to cook on that?' – pointing to my standard four-ring stove. However, he still managed to produce the most amazing beef consommé I have ever tasted.

The design of a kitchen should start with what, and how, you like to cook. If, for example, you are not terribly keen on cooking, you could limit the number and size of appliances you invest in. Maybe you love to cook while chatting to others, in which case a breakfast bar or other form of seating could be a congenial addition. Perhaps you like to combine cooking with dining, a common arrangement that makes the most of space and is nicely informal. (But in that case, you must always include a way of obscuring unwashed pots and pans. Viewed from the dining table, they are just too vivid a reminder of the washing-up chores to be done after you have deliciously indulged.)

When the weather is warm, it is wonderful to be able to cook outside. You could even invest in an 'outdoor kitchen' and a range barbecue that is specially designed for outdoor use. A much simpler alternative is a charcoal barbecue, which always gives food cooked outside the best flavour. Another idea is a wood-burning oven, in which to cook pizza and bread. They are not all that difficult to build and are quite a taste revelation.

If you do want to cook outside, life will be much easier if your outdoor cooking facilities are near the kitchen, so that you retain easy access to the refrigerator, sink and implements. The architect John Pawson has designed a kitchen for himself in which the cabinets and countertop were continued outside to create a beautifully sinuous outdoor kitchen.

Sometimes kitchens need to be less conspicuous, such as if they are situated in an open-plan room or a very small space. The concept of a 'kitchen in a cupboard' is a neat solution, and it has recently become possible to buy ready-made versions, obviating the call to the carpenter and complicated instructions.

LAYOUT

Whether a kitchen is built-in or freestanding, received wisdom rules that the 'work triangle' – in which the sink, range and refrigerator triangulate a given space – is the best layout. As with all 'rules', especially in design, one size does not always fit all.

The application of the work triangle will depend on the space available and your personal preference, especially as hobs (cooktops) and ovens can be independent items. There are some guidelines, however, that should not be ignored:

□ Try to leave at least 400mm (15³/4in) between lower and upper cabinets or shelves.

□ Avoid siting your oven or hob next to the refrigerator or freezer, otherwise these will have to use more energy to stay cool, unless you heavily insulate between the two.

□ Locate electrical sockets (outlets) at least 300mm (12in) away from the rim of the kitchen sink.

□ Install only finishes that are hardwearing and can be easily cleaned.

□ Fit child locks on cabinet doors, drawers and ovens to prevent little fingers from being injured. An induction hob will automatically turn itself off as soon as it is out of use, so is the most child-safe choice.

□ Locate the waste bins and sink next to the dishwasher, so tableware can be

scraped and rinsed before being loaded in the machine.

□ It is a good idea to keep a small fire extinguisher or fire blanket in a kitchen, next to the stove – think about the best place to keep this when devising your layout.

□ A double sink allows you to drain liquids in one if the other is full.

□ Trays can be quite bulky to store. A recess between lower cabinets is a handy solution. This is also a good way to store chopping boards and baking trays.

□ If you are planning a built-in kitchen, note that standard cabinet sizes are normally 900mm (35¹/2in) high by 600mm (24in) deep, in varying widths such as 300mm (12in), 400mm (15³/4in), 500mm (19³/4in), 800mm (31¹/2in) and 1000mm (39¹/2in).

It is always nice to be able to look out of a window while washing dishes. Ideally your windowsill should be above your lower cabinets, but this is not always possible, in which case freestanding versions can be fitted in front. However, make sure that your countertop incorporates a rear upstand

to stop things, including water, from disappearing down the back.

In a very small kitchen you will need to allow space for doors to open – on cabinets, refrigerator, dishwasher, and so on – as well as space for someone standing in front. Allow a minimum clearance space equal to the width of the door plus 700mm (27¹/2in).

03

01

A classic galley-style kitchen, where the window is left unobscured and the cheery yellow cabinets are confined to the long sides.

02

This island unit cleverly demarcates cooking and leg-swinging snacking, while also providing storage above.

03

An outdoor cooking area can be whatever you want it to be. Here in this olive grove it is a stone sink, a plank of wood, a few bricks and a couple of gas rings.

04

The designers of this kitchen have used fitted and unfitted elements to create a sharp but relaxed style that provides plenty of functionality while preserving the airy proportions of the given space.

04

01

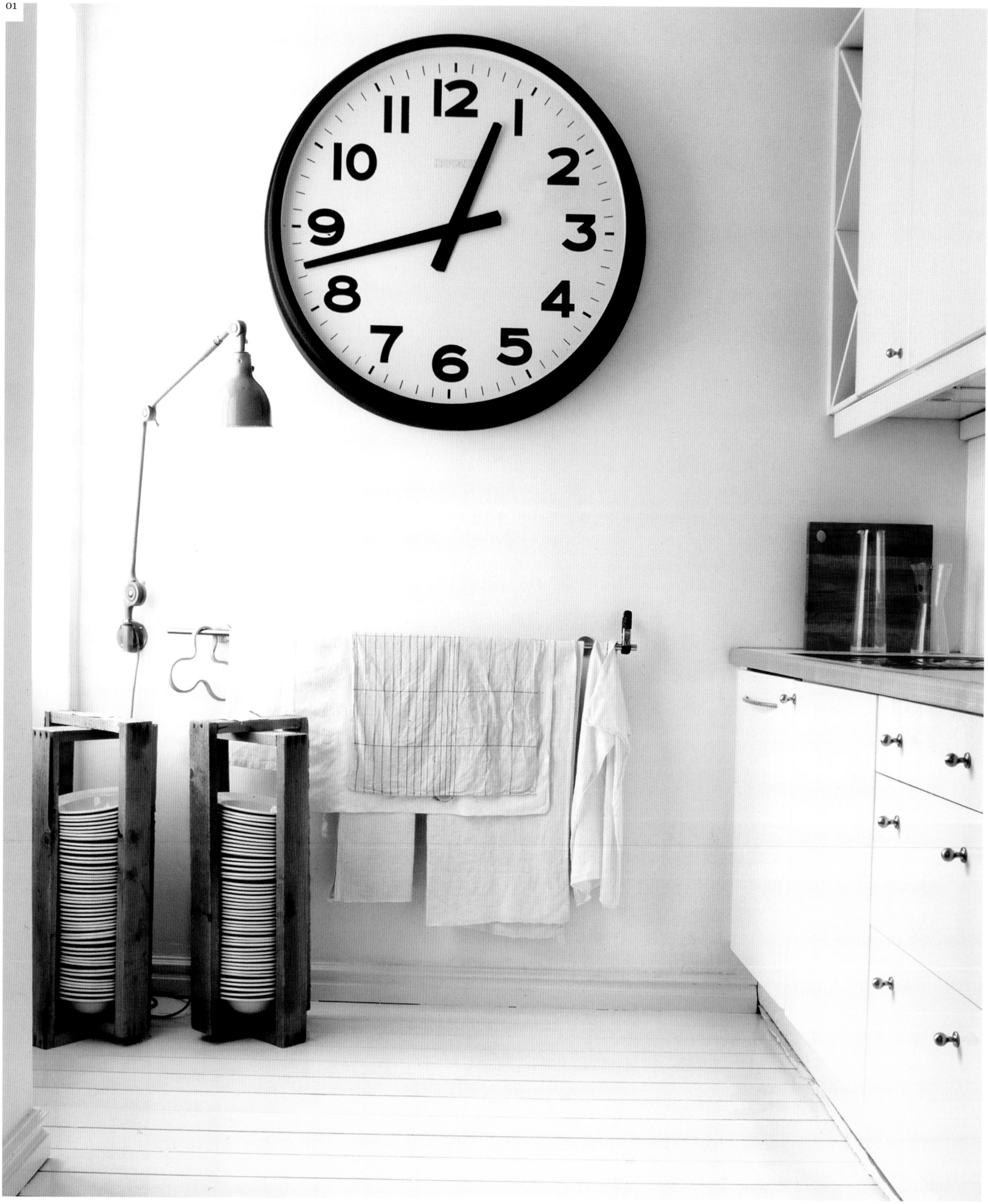

01
Tea towels and plates are displayed with an artistic eye.

02
This deeply attractive cooking and dining area mixes disciplined display with surfaces of handmade tiles, while using carefully selected textiles, furniture and light fittings to create a quietly dramatic space.

01

The area around a very standard hob (cooktop) and oven combination is made easier to use with a recessed shelf behind for oils and spices.

02

Appliances, such as the ovens shown here, are integrated and wholly recessive in this masterfully crafted kitchen.

03

The aga range gets top billing in this kitchen.

APPLIANCES

The appliances you choose, and the way you want to use them, will substantially determine their layout, but because, these days, appliances are able to perform such a wide variety of functions, choosing between them can be confusing. If you are not an enthusiastic cook, a straightforward gas or electric hob (cooktop) plus a combination oven (which allows you to cook with the speed of a microwave and the browning capability of a conventional oven) will probably suit you.

Hobs (cooktops)

Gas hobs tend to be the cook's favourite because they respond immediately when the flame is turned up or down. Electric hobs can be ceramic or induction, though they tend to look the same, finished in sheets of black glass. There are two kinds of ceramic hob: radiant and halogen. Halogen is faster than radiant – as fast as gas. Induction hobs are activated by

magnetism and require special pans; the heat will automatically shut off as soon as a pan is removed.

One innovation that can provide a wide range of functions is the domino hob, so called because the format looks like a domino, being one half of a conventional four-ring hob. A domino hob can include two induction rings and two gas rings; or two rings with an integrated deep-fat fryer, or a teppanyaki grill (allowing pan-free frying), or a chargrill, or a wok burner.

Ovens

Ovens, too, offer different functions. Dual-fuel ovens utilize both gas and electricity. Steam ovens are said to make meals extra moist; the steam comes from a reservoir of water that has to be topped up but does not have to be plumbed in. Convection fans distribute the heat evenly in the oven by means of a built-in fan. Infrared grills will quickly sear food. In small spaces, compact

ovens can be useful. Double ovens mean you can cook different things at different temperatures at the same time. It is also possible to source extra-large ovens, handy for the Christmas turkey. Ranges combine a hob with an oven, and some cast-iron varieties, like Agas and Rayburns, can heat hot water, too.

Perhaps the best way to discover what will suit you is to take a cooking course where you can try out different methods. Some suppliers run courses for just this purpose. Whatever you choose, allow at least 400mm (15¾in) countertop space – preferably heatproof – on each side of a hob and heatproof countertop space immediately adjacent to the oven, on which to place hot dishes.

If you choose to separate oven(s) and hob, it usually makes sense for them to be in close proximity. You may want to consider raising an oven to around countertop height, to avoid having to bend over.

Extractor fans

The designs of extractor fans are many and various, designed for different situations. Most can be either ducted, so that cooking smoke, grease and odours are deposited outside, or recirculating, where smoke, grease and odours are eliminated by filters. Filters must be washed or replaced regularly to maintain effectiveness. I have found that ducted designs tend to perform the best.

Telescopic and canopy fans can be integrated into wall-mounted cabinets and extended to 'catch' grease and smoke when cooking. Chimney fans are exposed and fitted against a wall, like a chimney. Island fans are designed to be mounted on a ceiling only.

Whichever you choose, ensure that there is clearance between the heat source and the base of the fan – of 650mm (25$\frac{1}{2}$in) if you are using gas to cook with, or of 400mm (15$\frac{3}{4}$in) if you are using electricity.

There are also down-draught fans that can be counter-mounted. These are relatively new to the market and still quite expensive, but because they are recessed into the countertop and then raised during operation, they can be the least intrusive.

Dishwashers

Dishwashers can be quite inefficient in their use of water, but dishwasher drawers can be a good solution, allowing for more limited cycles when you do not have as much to clean. Likewise, a single drawer, compact or slimline dishwasher is a good idea in a single-person household if washing dishes is not your thing, or in a small kitchen. You may consider raising a usually floor-mounted dishwasher to make it easier to access.

Refrigerators and freezers

Just as dishwashers are available in easy-to-access and highly flexible drawer formats, so, too, are refrigerators and freezers. Alternatively, you could choose an under-counter version or a full-height, extra-wide, family-size design, depending on how much you wish to keep cold. An indulgent arrangement is to have a fridge for food and a separate one for drinks. If you want a cold-water dispenser or an ice-cube maker, it will need to be plumbed in. If you love wine, you may also want to incorporate a wine cooler into your cooking area.

Make sure your refrigerator or freezer is perfectly level, or the doors will not close properly. This can be done using the adjustors in the feet, unless your floor is very uneven, in which case you may need to take extra measures.

In a very streamlined kitchen, these appliances can be completely integrated into the cabinets, with decorative front panels matching the cabinets, and will be designed for just this purpose, being slightly shallower. In a freestanding kitchen, the aesthetics of the appliances are important, so give some thought to their colour, material and shape.

LIGHTING AND ELECTRICITY

Very good task lighting is essential in the kitchen. Ceiling-mounted spotlights, recessed or surface-mounted, are popular, as they provide strong and focused light but are far enough away from cooking not to become drenched in steam and grease. Covered fittings will give additional protection, and directional fittings mean you will be able to adjust lighting to avoid glare.

Under-cabinet lighting will provide more localized light, though beware of fittings reflecting in very glossy splashbacks. If they are not worthy of exposure, conceal them behind a diffusing panel. Extractor fans usually incorporate a light, too.

Lighting located inside cabinets with glazed doors will add to your overall lighting scheme, as well as helping you to uncover the contents. This arrangement will also make small kitchens look bigger.

Countertop electrical sockets will be required for smaller appliances such as toasters and food processors. One handy way of concealing them is on the underside of wall-mounted cabinets.

01
Kitchen lighting need not be dull. Here a vintage wall-mounted, swivelling light fitting illuminates the action, while paper pendants provide the atmosphere.

02
Concealed lighting above and beneath these curiously carved wall cabinets provides task and ambient illumination, amplified by the white cabinets and countertop below. An alluring space spiced up by the surprise of the red sink.

03
Size is more than compensated for by quality and individuality in this kitchen, which incorporates bespoke joinery and thoughtful artistry in its layout and design.

04
A reclaimed baker's trolley is the ideal place to store pots and pans.

STORAGE

Most kitchen storage takes the form of built-in cabinets, but freestanding storage such as armoires, dressers, chests of drawers or other individual pieces of furniture can be both capacious and versatile. An advantage of freestanding storage (and appliances) is that it can be taken with you when you move house.

Perishable food will usually be stored in a refrigerator, but if you live in a temperate climate and if an exterior north- or east-facing wall forms part of the perimeter of your cooking zone, you might want to consider installing an old-fashioned walk-in pantry with airbricks on the outside wall, which is an energy-free way of keeping things cool. You can store non-perishables here, too, including bulky items, which makes for easy access and relieves the cooking area of lots of cabinets.

Another idea is to clad an entire wall with floor-to-ceiling storage, including any refrigeration, and then hide it all with sliding doors. This is an increasingly common device in the most avant-garde Italian and German kitchens.

Cabinets with adjacent left- and right-opening doors and no central brace are good for storing and accessing large items. Deep, wide drawers with good, strong runners for pans and tableware are another easy-to-access alternative, though they need to incorporate rubber matting or pegs to stop the contents from sliding around. Glass or mesh doors add interest to a run of cabinets, though mesh does allow dust to penetrate.

Open shelving creates a lovely informal look, but exposed surfaces collect dust and grease and are therefore best for items you use often. If space is tight, a beautiful device is to fit glass shelves in front of a window, to store all your glassware. A single shallow shelf fitted just above the main countertop, for oils, spices and other small items, can be a helpful way of keeping countertops clutter-free.

03

04

01

A large sink, incorporating a drainer,
is complemented by simple
shelving immediately above and
a couple of handy tea towels to
the side, all wrapped up in a deep
and divine colour scheme.

COUNTERTOPS AND SINKS

For countertop material options, see Chapter 5, page 200. If you are a keen pastry-maker you will appreciate at least one section being made of marble. It can also be useful to integrate a wooden chopping board, while an integrated draining board will look slick. Countertops with slightly rounded corners will prevent adults from bruising their hips and children their foreheads.

Kitchen sink and tap (faucet) options are also covered in Chapter 5 (see pages 202–3). One factor that will affect your choice is the size of sink you want; do not forget that roasting pans, baking trays and suchlike can be quite large and still need washing, probably by hand. The other major factor is the style of the kitchen – integrated can be chic, while a more old-fashioned look, such as a ceramic Belfast (apron) sink, can be rustic and charming.

HEAT AND WASTE

Cooking requires heat, so if you can't stand the heat of the kitchen, you will need to make sure it is well ventilated. Windows and fans are low-tech options, while air conditioning and comfort-cooling are more radical solutions (see Chapter 7, pages 245–7).

Cooking also generates waste. Vegetable matter can be composted, along with paper and cardboard, and a small bin recessed into the countertop can be helpful. Non-vegetable matter can be recycled, but this can be messy, as well as space-consuming, so make adequate provision for this when drawing up your plans. Specialist compartmentalized recycling bins are designed to manage waste that will be collected, but you may want to make other arrangements for items you can reuse yourself, such as plastic bags or food containers.

TEA TOWELS AND COOKBOOKS

Tea towels need to go somewhere, so bear this in mind when planning. The oven handle is a popular spot, as towels also have a chance to dry, though this is considered a fire risk.

If you enjoy cooking, you will probably have cookbooks. These will need to go somewhere, so make provision in your plan, as countertop space for more than a couple of volumes will not do. Freestanding refrigerators often have space above them, which is ideal as a single shelf for books.

WINDOW TREATMENTS

Steam and grease will damage or soil most window dressings, so keep them to a minimum – a simple shade, for example – or opt for dressings that can be wiped down, such as a Venetian blind or plantation shutters. Remember that you will need to be able to open windows easily in a steamy or smoky atmosphere.

SHOPPING LISTS

A chalkboard makes it easy to keep a running shopping list, as it is big enough that you won't forget to write ingredients down as soon as you use them up. I usually end up painting the doors of electrical cupboards with chalkboard paint (which comes in a number of different colours as well as traditional black), making them instantly less intrusive and much more useful.

UPDATING

A kitchen can be as easily updated as any other space, perhaps even more so as there are more components to play with. Freshening up a single feature, whether flooring, wall finishes, countertops or cabinet doors, will transform the whole. Even just changing the hardware on the cabinets will make a big difference, much as a great piece of jewellery can transform a tired outfit.

dressing

The day I created a dressing room for myself was the day I felt truly grown up. It is all very well dressing and undressing in the bedroom, but if one of you is on an early flight or back late from a party, a dressing room makes life much more agreeable. Even a walk-in closet, which is essentially a mini dressing room, will suffice.

Sometimes none of these options are feasible. Unless you have a huge bedroom – in which case you may well have already hived off space for a dressing room – you will therefore need to be clever in the way you store your clothes, especially if there is more than one person's clothing to store.

01

02

FURNITURE

Built-in closets will always be more space-efficient than freestanding wardrobes and should be made to look as much like the adjacent walls as possible. To calculate how much wardrobe space you need, simply measure your clothes, allowing a drop of 1000mm (39½in) for separates, such as skirts and folded trousers, or shirts and blouses. Allow 1600mm (63in) for long dresses and 1400mm (55in) for coats. Wardrobes need to be at least 600mm (24in) deep to accommodate the span of hangers. Antique wardrobes are rarely this deep, so measure before you buy.

Also measure the height and width of folded items, and assess the mass and variation of underwear so that you can provide a drawer for each type. Count pairs of shoes, and if you are planning cubbyholes for them you will also need to check the height of your highest and lowest pairs. While boots can be stored below short hanging clothes, there is wisdom in storing all footwear separately – and in a well-ventilated unit. Bags can be stored on a shelf above a hanging rail or in their own cubbyholes. Ties and belts can be hung on the back of wardrobe doors, as can necklaces.

Add an extra 10 per cent to your calculations to allow for new purchases. If space is tight, especially lovely items could be displayed as decorative pieces, but this is unlikely to make much of a dent in your overall needs. What will make a big difference is if you archive your clothes seasonally. Winter clothes are always particularly bulky and can quite comfortably live out the summer in separate storage. Vacuum-pack sweaters, if possible, using your vacuum cleaner and specialist bags, or just pack them in plastic clothes bags.

To reduce the risk of moth damage wherever your clothes are, ensure they are scrupulously clean – moths especially love clothes dressed with the sharp sauce of human sweat. Liberally apply cotton sachets of cloves, lavender, rosemary, thyme, dried orange peel or cedar, which will also make your wardrobe smell divine. Avoid chemical mothballs at all costs: they stink, and, while lethal to moths, they are not especially healthy for humans or pets, either.

Dressing tables, and an accompanying stool, have enjoyed something of a renaissance over recent years and will add grace to any dressing area. They are also superbly multifunctional items, useful for storing smaller items of clothes or costume jewellery, as well as somewhere to do hair and makeup or display photographs and vases of flowers.

If there is no space for a table, then a solitary seat, such as a sculptural chair or a divan, will make putting shoes on and taking them off more comfortable. It also provides somewhere to discard clothes, though this is not to be encouraged unless you want your home to look like a laundry.

A laundry basket is helpful in a dressing area. Ideally it will be concealed, but if it is exposed it should look good – a beautiful basket, say. Having two laundry baskets will allow clothes to be pre-sorted for dry-cleaning and laundering.

Lighting and mirrors

Emulate the strong overhead lighting found in the fitting rooms of clothing stores. They have a vested interest in helping you properly see what you are wearing. If your dressing area is in your bedroom, however, make sure this overhead lighting is on a separate circuit to bedside or dressing-table lights.

A full-length three-way mirror is the best way to judge your appearance from all angles. An alternative is to fit the rear of two adjacent wardrobe doors (hinged at the outer edges) with mirrors, so that you can see yourself from all angles.

Jewellery

If you need to store valuable jewellery, sometimes the safest place is the least obvious. Consult security specialists with regard to fitting a safe, but you could also consider false compartments that can be incorporated into your dressing area. Or, better still, conceal a safe behind a false compartment.

Nakedness

To go barefoot in communal parts of your home, such as the kitchen or living room, is a matter of preference and even culture, but in a bathroom or dressing area it is an inevitability. Unlike in a bathroom, though, your choice of flooring is not limited by the presence of water, so do consider what you would like naked feet to feel.

Likewise, you will need to ensure that your dressing area benefits from plenty of light, especially daylight. However, you may not want to put on a peep show, in which case Venetian blinds or opaque voile curtains are a good solution.

01

Here the headboard cleverly doubles as storage, relieving the bedroom's perimeter of furniture.

02

03

04

02

A bank of integrated wardrobes in dark chocolate represents a good solution when there is simply not enough space for both a bedroom and a dressing room.

03

An oddly shaped space is transformed into a luxurious gentleman's dressing room through the imaginative combination of built-in and freestanding furniture

04

A vintage dressing table is attractive and always appealing.

eating and drinking

The writer Virginia Woolf said, 'One cannot think well, love well, sleep well, if one has not dined well' – and to dine well it helps to do so in a well-designed spot. Some reports have indicated that as many as 75 per cent of families watch television while eating, and it is commonplace for family members to eat separately from one another, in rooms ranging from the bedroom to the living room. Eating habits such as these are not psychologically healthy, compromising social development in children and the cohesion of the family unit.

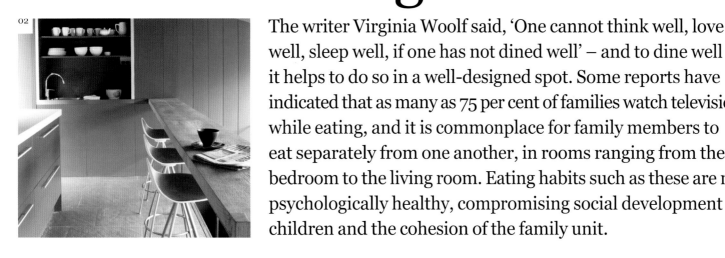

01
The theatrical juxtaposition of the period of this room and the period of the furniture and lighting installed creates an exciting dining space.

02
This intriguing kitchen not only features a recessed sink but contrasts rough with smooth in the choice of material for the bar.

Creating an alluring and comfortable space to eat in, therefore, is as much a matter of wellbeing as simple aesthetics. Dining can take many forms, though, depending on your personal preferences and the occasion.

You might like to occasionally grab quick bites in the kitchen, in which case a small seating area will suit – either a little table and chairs or an extension to the countertop with a couple of bar stools. Eating in the kitchen instead of having a separate dining room is also space-efficient and means you do not have quite so far to schlep laden with plates, although separating the dining area from the kitchen upstairs imparts a perhaps not unwelcome degree of formality.

Where a dining area is separate from the kitchen it should be located in close proximity – a serving hatch between the kitchen and dining space can be invaluable. Hatches have been 'uncool' for so long that they are becoming 'cool' again. If you don't agree, you could conceal it behind a handsome armoire – open the doors to reveal the hatch behind. If distance is unavoidable, a device such as a hostess trolley (wheeled cart), a hot tray or a dumbwaiter may be required.

In some of the homes I have designed I have been very lucky to have enough space to accommodate both formal and informal dining areas. This gives maximum flexibility in the design of each room and allows the formal dining area to be dramatized in ways that would not necessarily be practical in kitchen/diner surroundings, such as using very low lighting or lots of plush surfaces.

01
This extra-long dining table indicates a generous host and one with an eye for stimulating scale.

02
Rustic and contemporary are at play in this dining space, where furniture placed at the perimeter serves to support the main event.

03
This glossy white dresser supports a mirror that reflects atmospheric candlelight back into the dining space beyond.

04
A chalkboard-topped table makes dining for children just that little bit more fun.

FURNITURE

Good posture is essential to good digestion, so even if you are mixing furniture pieces ensure that chair and table heights match up. A standard tabletop height is 740mm (29in), for which a good seat height is 440mm (17 ¼in). Similarly, if you are creating a little breakfast bar make sure that the heights of surfaces match with bar stools. A standard bar stool height is 740mm (29in), which means a good bar height is around 1040mm (41in). A foot rail makes sitting on the stool a great deal more comfortable.

If you have small children, highchairs in garish colours are not entirely necessary; it is possible to source one that will share the more adult aesthetics of your other dining chairs. Make sure that the chair is entirely steady and will contain the child safely and comfortably. Alternatively, a good-quality booster seat fitted to a regular chair will suffice. If you have the space, a miniature children's table and chairs can be charming and are useful for other activities.

Eating outdoors will usually require a dedicated set of dining furniture, though not always: I have designed tables on wheels that can be pushed outside on sunny days. This is a good solution for small terraces, but any pendant lighting will need to be retractable, so that you do not end up walking into low-slung pendant shades. It helps if there is no step between inside and outside.

It can be useful to have an additional surface from which to serve: a credenza (a long side cabinet with shelves at each end), sideboard or side table works well. The benefit of a sideboard or a credenza is that it can also tidy away accessories such as table linen, cutlery (flatware), china, glassware and cruets, which will be particularly important in more formal dining spaces, including those that are open to living spaces.

If you have lovely-looking accessories, you might want to consider storing them in a vitrine, a posh word for a glass-fronted cabinet, so that they are on display for you to admire. Internal lighting will add drama to your lighting scheme.

01

Drinks

Drinking needs no equipment, other than a vessel from which to drink. Drinks are another matter. Perhaps you would prefer to keep all drinks in a refrigerator or pantry in the kitchen. An ice-maker here can create a lot more ice for you than a few trays in the freezer compartment.

If you love good wine you could keep it in a special, temperature-controlled wine cabinet, but wine can also be stored on racks, so long as the temperature is not too high or variable. It is best stored at about 12°C (54°F) out of direct sunlight, out of any draughts, and nowhere near a source of heat such as an oven, dishwasher or radiator. Bear in mind that wine racks can take up a lot of space. You need to allow for a height and width of 100mm (4in) and a depth of 350mm (14in) for each bottle, plus the width of the frame.

If you would prefer a cellar, but do not have one already, it is possible to avoid digging out the basement and instead sink a spiral cellar into the ground. This vertical concrete tunnel, about 2m (6ft 6in) wide and between 2m (6ft 6in) and 3m (10ft) deep, contains a downward-spiralling wine rack, with access via a trapdoor.

Artistically illuminated wine displays in dining areas can be all that is needed to create an inviting atmosphere. But if wine is to be stored there permanently, follow the above guidelines.

Lighting

Lighting in a dining area is obviously important from a practical point of view – you need to be able to see what you are eating and drinking. But it is equally important to consider the atmosphere it creates, as mood will inescapably influence satisfaction.

Pendant light fittings suspended over a table provide localized light that is both practical and seductive. The fittings should be suspended 70–80cm (27½–31½in) above the table. Should you wish to suspend a pendant any higher, consider including a diffuser to conceal the light bulb. But remember, the closer a fitting is to the table, the greater the sense of intimacy.

playing

Play should not be the preserve of small children, though they do tend to lead the field. Child's play can develop imagination, social skills, self-awareness and language skills, and encourage discovery of the world around the child. In the same way, 'play' for older children and adults has been proved to sharpen skills and express creativity, ultimately resulting in stress-relief – so, making provision for play in a home is extremely worthwhile.

The first step is to establish how your household likes to play, though the fullest expression of the answer might yet be unknown. In that case it could be time to take some courses to learn new, enjoyable skills.

It is not necessary to create dedicated 'play space' in the form of a playroom, den, media room, hobby room, dark room, studio or even a home gym. Rarely will homes have the capacity anyhow, but accommodating play somehow will make life much more pleasurable generally and make activities more effective.

Children's play space should always feature sufficient storage to allow all toys to be tidied away at the end of the day. If the play space is in a living room, the storage should be in the same style as the living room, not the toys.

Wall and floor surfaces should be wipe-clean but soft enough not to graze, and a little table and chairs at child height will always be useful. If space is tight the table could be hinged to the wall and folded away when not in use, and the chairs hung on pegs on the wall.

A home gym can be incorporated into a dressing room or guest room. Guest rooms always make useful hobby rooms or dens. As in all multifunctional spaces, storage is the key to true effectiveness, so that one activity need not intrude on another.

Converting an attic or shed into 'play space' means you do not need to deal with the demands of multiple functions. But a successful space will still depend on a combination of sufficient, well-ordered storage, easy-to-maintain fittings and surfaces, and good lighting.

01

01
A staircase becomes a slide.

02
A hallway becomes a (French) playground.

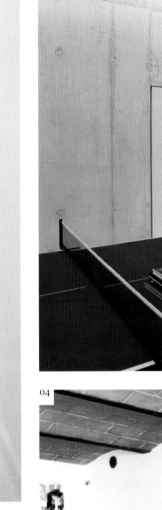

03
A kitchen/dining space with a multifunctional table, including table tennis.

04
A place for hobbies is serviced by ample desktop storage and two enchanting chandeliers.

01

A handy hammock, redolent of
sunny vacations, is slung across
a living room to provide both a
resting place and personality.

01

02

There is something about a
swinging seat that has back-to-
the-womb appeal.

03

An odd corner has been converted
into a substantial library. Note the
cute inset in the bottom step and
the chandelier and shelving in the
same blue as the sky above.

02

03

resting

Rest is not simply relaxation. Certain activities can be relaxing – hiking or computer gaming, for example – but they are not necessarily restful. Nor does rest mean sleep, though the effects can be similar. Resting is when our minds and bodies are passive, though not inactive.

Reading is one passive activity that can be restful, though perhaps the ultimate kind of rest is when we allow our minds to wander. We may have some of our best ideas when we least expect them – in the bath or sitting on a train, perhaps. The prolific painter Leonardo da Vinci subscribed to just this idea. When clients complained he was wasting time by resting on the bed in his studio he retorted, 'If I don't do this, you don't get the work.'

Science has proved that resting is essential. If we do not rest, the brain takes it by force, resulting in lack of concentration or even mental breakdown. Rest days are often important in religion, where the limit on physical activity is intended to promote reflection, contemplation and meditation. Likewise, rest is essential to building up physical strength. The most effective training is always tempered by a period of rest and recuperation.

If reading is the way in which you can rest most effectively, then perhaps you should consider installing a library, or simply a specific reading corner, with a comfortable chair and a good directional light. Shelves tailored to the height of books always look the smartest. If you find listening to music particularly restful, why not invest in a high-quality music system?

A well-positioned day bed, chaise longue or hammock will couch thoughtful moments, but in order to be productive they must be protected, even isolated, from other more noisy and active parts of your home. Peace is what is needed for rest.

sharing

Pets are a comfort; the clue, after all, is in the name. They are scientifically proved to relieve stress, and dogs in particular encourage healthy exercise with their need for regular walking. Surveys have even found that a surprisingly high percentage of single people have replaced their partner with a pet.

01

02

01
A playful, cosy hideaway for dog,
or child.

02
Pet accessories need not be
unattractive: this macaw is at
home on his antique stand in front
of the antique vitrine and pots.

03
A tank of tropical fish, fitted flush
into the wall, is one of a number of
curious elements in this eclectic
dining room.

04
Dogs love to sleep beneath
something, and this spot under
the wellington boots is ideal.
And when he needs to take his
owners for walkies, their lead
is close to hand.

Pets don't always pay close attention to style,
however. If you have spent time and effort on
making your home gorgeous, it is a shame
to have it compromised by ill-considered
pet paraphernalia. Equally, it seems to
me that there is something disrespectful
to your pet if no effort is made to weave
their quarters into the weft of your home,
as if they are just a temporary intrusion.

Thankfully, there are myriad sources
of well-designed pet accessories – from
birdcages to dog beds and even cat litter
trays – which should be indestructible and
easy to clean, as well as comfortable and
good-looking. Remember to incorporate
storage for all those items that need not be
on show, such as food, treats and toys. A
pretty basket with a lid would be satisfactory.

As regards to human furniture to
which pets have access, you may want
to consider slipcovers for protection.
Steer clear of very dark or very light
colours, as these will show up fur and
marks very easily. If your pets chew or
scratch your furniture it is because they
are bored or distressed, not just because
your choices are delicious.

03

04

sleeping

Sleep hygiene – that is, getting enough sleep – is essential to good health and yet there are so many things that can intrude. Sound, light, temperature, humidity and the quality of your bed can all conspire to keep you awake. Fortunately, all these problems can be solved with good design.

The first rule is never to locate work or any kind of onerous activity in a bedroom. A television is also inadvisable, though very popular; a good read is far more effective at slowing brain activity in readiness for sleep.

01

01
This chaise longue is an inviting
spot for an afternoon nap.

02
Interlined, full-length curtains and
carpets in this bedroom make for
a quiet sleeping space.

FURNITURE

The perfect bed is both comfortable and
supportive and, according to some studies,
can result in extra sleep. For tips on how
to choose the perfect bed see page 214.

A bedside table or night stand with a
drawer will be the most useful. If there
is only space for a small and therefore
lightweight table, a wall-mounted design
is less likely to be accidentally knocked over.

WINDOW TREATMENTS

If the creep of daylight is unwelcome,
window treatments that comprehensively
block out daylight are essential. The
failsafe solution consists of a combination
of double-lined curtains with a blackout
shade mounted behind. Blackout shades
alone, as their name suggests, can also be
effective, but bear in mind that light can
still ooze around the edges. Another solution
is plantation shutters.

This white and charcoal bedroom is illuminated by a combination of simple side lights and a decorative chandelier.

02
Like a rich fruitcake this bedroom mixes a variety of textures and tastes into one delicious space; the bedside here is unusually illuminated by a swivelling light fitting on the perpendicular wall.

01
Wall-mounted bedside tables, such as the ones in this bedroom, are a good solution when space is limited, as are the wall-mounted bedside lights.

02
The vibrant effect of hard walls and floor is softened by lined, voluminous silk curtains.

03
This mirrored headboard acts as both decorative feature and light source, as it will sparkle once the bedside lamps are switched on.

04
The occupants of this bedroom benefit from the flexibility of having the television on show or not, fitted as it is within a wardrobe.

Sound

Sleep can also be disturbed by sound (though scientific studies have concluded that absolute quiet can be just as disturbing). If your home is located on a busy street you would be well advised to site your bedroom at the opposite end of the building. Alternatively, install well-insulated windows and heavy curtains. Soft surfaces will all contribute to the ideal soporific cocoon: upholstered walls and even ceilings, and carpeted floors or deep-pile rugs, which also feel pleasing to naked feet.

Temperature and humidity

Coolness and controlled humidity are as essential to good sleep as the absence of daylight and sound. Ensure that any heat sources can be properly regulated and that ventilation is effective. In very dry climates you may need a humidifier, which should be as unobtrusive as possible. For further details see Chapter 7, pages 245–7.

Bedding

Bedding needs to be stored somewhere in your home, and your bedroom may be the best, or even the only available, place. Consider a blanket box at the end of your bed and allow for this when drawing up your plan. Alternatively, a bed with storage beneath is a popular solution.

Lighting

Even if there is overhead lighting in a bedroom, it should be supplemented by bedside lighting in the form of either table lamps or wall lights, which are less easy to knock over, on a separate lighting circuit. The lower edge of the shade should be at eye-level when you are sitting in bed.

Directional fittings will help focus light onto a book without disturbing your partner too much. And bedside switches, which can turn off all the lights in a room, mean you will not have to propel yourself out of a warm bed to turn all the lights off.

Privacy

A sense of privacy and security is important to the ability to sleep well. Something as simple as a door lock can help in this respect.

Napping

Planned daytime naps can improve alertness without necessarily affecting nocturnal sleep. If you are a 'napper', or would like to be, consider incorporating into your home spots where you can blissfully nap – perhaps a chaise longue in a dressing room, as opposed to the more nocturnal environs of a bedroom?

01

02

04

03

socializing

Different cultures socialize in different ways. Those who live in countries with cool or unpredictable climates tend to socialize more at home. With this in mind I have designed many homes with both private and formal living rooms, locating the television in the private space and investing in more elegant or dramatic furnishings to suit more formal or stimulating surroundings.

01
Extra seating can be provided by these space efficient velvet-covered benches.

Indulgence like this is not always possible, but can be compensated for by clever design that is multifunctional and flexible enough to provide for extra bodies.

In a living room little stools and ottomans can provide additional seating, and a classic nest of tables will do the rest. I have designed large occasional tables with small stools stored beneath for just this purpose.

Hiding the television
A focal point, such as a fireplace, painting or picture window will always make a living room more congenial. The television should not be the focal point – if the living room is where you watch television, it should ideally be concealed, as it will probably jar and be distracting in company, even when it is turned off.

Ready-made TV cabinets are rarely attractive, nor are they likely to suit the rest of your decor – this is where custom furniture is well worth the investment. Be sure to allow sufficient air to circulate around the television, as it can become very hot. Your supplier will be able to advise you on minimum ventilation requirements.

One neat design that has become popular is the TV lift, whereby the television is submerged into a short floor-mounted cabinet. An alternative is to customize an existing piece of cabinetry, such as an armoire. Or fit a mirror or painting on a sash- (double-hung-) window mechanism that can be drawn over a recessed screen.

Flexible dining areas
Dining spaces should be accommodating to your social life, with plenty of space to sit and eat comfortably. An extending dining table, with extra chairs stored at the sides of the room, is a classic solution. The Shakers cleverly allowed for extra guests by hanging spare chairs on wall-mounted pegs. And the designers Precious McBane designed a beautiful bespoke dining table with a base that could contain extra folding chairs. Benches can be flexible, seating as many as can squeeze on, but a seat without a back will be less comfortable than one with a back.

If your dining room is your home office, there should be not a trace of evidence when guests are around. You and they will be much more relaxed as a result.

A social ambience

Amusing decor and, most importantly, flattering lighting in all the spaces where you entertain will create an alluring mix. After all, you want to create a relaxing ambience, not inspect complexions.

To this end I rarely see the point of overhead lighting in a living room. A combination of table lamps, floor lamps and wall lights will always be a more seductive solution. They can all be turned on and off with a switch at the entrance to make life a little easier.

A really fabulous and social thing to do is to include a bar somewhere. This need not be the kitsch 1950s kind, shaped like a boat that has washed up in your home, but simply a cupboard with pocket doors that recede to reveal all the elements a good bar needs. A little sink, a small refrigerator and an ice-maker will all be useful additions.

Music

Music will always get a party going, so consider having a good hi-fi system. Decide on the best location for this, including the speakers, ideally before you have final finishes installed so that you can conceal any wiring.

Musical instruments such as pianos and cellos can be bulky, but if they are to be accommodated you will need to find space. Measure the full area required when the instrument is in use and incorporate this into your scale plan. Avoid siting them next to radiators or in direct sunshine.

01
A vintage sideboard becomes a
conveniently placed bar.

02
The black and white colour scheme
and graphic shapes help make the TV
disappear and stop it from dominating
an otherwise social space.

03
A pull-down bed is a space-efficient
way to accommodate guests.

Guest bedrooms and bathrooms

Always use guest accommodation yourself
so that you can solve anything that does not
work or is uncomfortable before guests are
installed. If a guest bedroom has to double
as a dressing room, home gym or home
office, well-thought-out storage will be
essential so that one function does not
intrude on the other.

The market offers a good choice of
space-friendly beds. These range from a
sofa bed to a fold-away bed that folds up
against the wall and can even be concealed
in a cupboard, or a rise-and-fall bed that
converts from a single to a double bed.

In children's bedrooms I nearly always
install bunk beds with a trundle bed below,
as sleepovers are an essential part of
childhood. Make sure that bunk beds are
safe; the top bunk should not be used by
very young children.

03

storing

Something as prosaic as storage can be the secret to a happy home, particularly if shared. Depending on the size of a home and the amount of possessions, storage can liberate space from the congesting flotsam and jetsam of life, so that it can be more comfortably, and even more safely, lived in. For this reason adequate storage is essential in a home of limited size whose occupants are not sworn ascetics. Possessions also become much easier to find when items are clearly separated.

Assessing your needs

Storage can be divided into two categories: short-term and long-term. Short-term storage needs to be instantly accessible, whereas reduced accessibility can be tolerated in long-term storage, for example in an attic.

To estimate accurately how much storage space you need, measure the mass of what you want to store and then add a 'future-proofing' contingency of at least 10 per cent. Grouping items by frequency of usage and function will help you to identify not only the capacity of storage you need but the best location for it, too. Units with compartments and adjustable shelves will help you to separate items so that you don't have to rummage around looking for them.

What you want to store will influence whether you choose enclosed or unenclosed storage – the difference between, say, a chest of drawers and open shelves. Enclosed storage is the obvious choice for items that need to be kept out of sight or protected from dust, but consideration must be given to the threat of pests and humidity. If your items are at risk of theft, security measures will need to be incorporated into your chosen solution, from locks to hidden compartments (see page 249).

01
An undulating matrix of solids and voids creates a sculptural storage solution and space divider.

02
Reclaimed wooden lockers artfully store and display an osseous collection.

03
A storage wall offers cupboards and bookshelves, and an almost secret door, too.

01

01

A fresh take on an under-stairs cupboard, where the material and form of the doors echoes the same qualities in the banister behind.

02

Pink Perspex (Plexiglas) is used to create attention-grabbing storage that still acknowledges the benefits of flowing light and space.

03

An architectural feature reveals its true function.

Customizing

Freestanding storage such as cabinets and chests may provide you with sufficient capacity, but built-in storage is the most space-efficient solution. It will tailor itself both to the contours of your home and to the objects to be stored, to capitalize on every nook and cranny.

In a room with mouldings, the fascia of any full-height and full-width built-in storage should be given the same mouldings, to make it 'disappear' into the background. The same applies to the finish – built-in storage should match that of adjacent walls, or make a noticeably contrasting statement.

For enclosed storage in a limited space, consider cabinets with pocket doors, or tambours. These recess and therefore require less clearance when open.

Children's items

Babies and children are renowned for generating a lot of 'stuff', the permanent display of which is rarely desirable in the home. Larger items can often be stored in an under-stairs cupboard, but if there is no room these items could be suspended from wall-mounted hooks, so long as there is sufficient clearance around them.

Involving children in how they store their possessions is a good foundation for engaging them with the space in which they live. It will also mean you have some help when it is time to tidy up. Toys and dressing-up clothes should always be stored away in boxes. Your home will then be tidy and there will be no danger of twisted ankles.

Outside help

You may discover that there are some items for which you simply do not have adequate space, so you could consider storing these in a garden shed. Even a wall-mounted 'mini-shed' on a balcony will help. This solution, however, is obviously only suitable for items that will not be significantly affected by changes in temperature and humidity, are resistant to possible infestation, are easy to clean and can be easily secured. In the absence of any suitable outdoor storage space, items that you do not need every day and that you find are compromising the day to day fluid functioning of your home could be placed in professional storage away from the home.

working

An otherwise almost unusable
nook is converted into an invaluable
work space through imaginative
use of a layout on the diagonal.

Working from home is not a new phenomenon. The Medici, the Renaissance banking family, pioneered double-entry book-keeping from the comfort of their lavish palaces in Florence; and the business of British colonies was largely conducted from the ground-floor rooms of city town houses. Even manufacturing initially occurred as 'cottage industry', but the Industrial Revolution excised both industry and commerce from the domestic realm.

The post-Industrial Revolution, wrought by advances in communications technology – principally the internet – has allowed us to work from home once again. However, the intervening isolation of the office has taught valuable lessons in optimizing the working environment, lessons that can be applied back to today's home office. For example, the positive effect of control over one's work space on productivity is nowhere more fully exercised than in the home.

LOOK AND FEEL

Even if we do not perform paid work from home, the management of any household involves paperwork. Traditionally such domestic clerical tasks were serviced by a 'bureau', an indispensable piece of furniture. Its title discreetly conveyed its purpose and its design language chimed with the domestic environments of the day, yet it still contained an efficient labyrinth of variously sized compartments as well as a pull-out or pull-down writing surface. All could be securely locked away once letters had been written and bills paid.

This principle of harmonizing work space with home space, by minimizing the visual intrusion of work-related equipment, is worthy of imitation. This way there is total control over look and feel, so long as practical considerations are taken into account. The alternative is to select equipment as much for its aesthetics as its function.

01
A traditional home office consisting of a capacious bureau. The pictures, lamps and wall colour make for a charming ensemble.

02
A home office can be closed off and hidden behind concertina sliding doors at the end of a working day.

03
A contemporary take on the traditional bureau, which is disguised as an attractive living-room cabinet once the laptop is stowed away.

LOCATION

The home office is likely to be accommodated in one of three ways:

☐ In a separate, dedicated room. This is the ideal scenario, where a doorway preserves the psychologically necessary threshold between work life and domestic life, ensuring privacy and security, too.

☐ In a separate room that is also occasionally required to perform another function. It is common to locate a home office in a little-used dining room or guest bedroom, for example. Well-designed storage that can be closed off will be essential to seamless multifunctionality, concealing all evidence of work when the secondary function is in play, except, perhaps, for 'neutral' objects such as books. For instance, a notice board can be discreetly mounted on the inside of a cupboard door.

☐ In a regularly used area of the home. The need for well-judged concealment applies even more urgently to a home office located in a well-used part of the home, such as the kitchen or living room. A bureau-style approach, either freestanding or built-in, is highly appropriate. This will fulfil required functions but also be sympathetic to the style of the rest of the home, while concealing the detritus of work.

Whichever of these options is open to you, the practicalities requiring consideration remain the same. These range from the choice of furniture, storage and lighting to ways of dealing with technological and security needs.

FURNITURE

It is not necessary to work at a desk per se. All you really need is a work surface at a suitable height: 750mm (29in) is standard. If space allows, a secondary surface is always useful, where clutter can be centralized, leaving as much as possible of the main work surface clear.

Nor is it necessary to invest in a desk chair, so long as your chair conforms to the following ergonomic advice. This is important, to avoid the injuries typically resulting from sitting at a desk for prolonged periods of time. (In fact, the best desk chairs are designed specifically with these factors in mind.)

☐ Your feet should be able to rest on the floor without dangling.

☐ There should be sufficient clearance between the front of your seat and the back of your knees.

☐ The front edges of the seat should ideally be padded.

☐ The seat cushion should be firm; a slight contour is ideal.

☐ The backrest should support the lumbar region – the five lower segments of the spine should be in constant contact.

☐ A chair with a high back should also support your neck.

☐ Armrests should be adjustable in height, so that your shoulders are not forced to hunch.

☐ If you use a computer, the top of the monitor should be at eye-level, and your forearms should be parallel to the floor when using the keyboard.

01

TECHNOLOGY

In this age of wireless technology it is becoming less necessary to use cables to connect a computer to ancillary equipment – printer, scanner, fax machine, router – but this facility is not yet universally enjoyed. If you are surrounded by cables, a small hole in the work surface next to your computer, through which you can feed the cables (rather than shoving them across and down the back of your desk) is ideal. Just make sure you also fit a cable-management collar, so that you don't lose little things, such as erasers and coins, down the hole.

Though there are notable exceptions, most ancillary equipment is not pretty and so should be concealed, or at least discreetly tucked away. A separate shelving unit with sized-to-fit pigeonholes would be a good option. But it is obviously important that equipment is accessible, and also the electrical and telecom sockets into which machines are plugged.

If you are designing a home office from scratch, take the opportunity to fit additional sockets (outlets) in close proximity to your equipment, minimizing the inevitable 'cat's cradle' of cables. Consider also the need to recharge mobile telephones, MP3 players and PDAs. You may need more sockets than you originally thought.

01
Work spaces can be made into
fun spaces, too, a fact fully
recognized by the work-from-
home designer who operates
from this office space.

02
A row of tea chests beneath a
cacophony of curios and carefully
pinned drawings suggest both an
ordered and inventive mind is at
work here.

Light

A good source of natural light in the home office, such as a window or even a glazed door, is healthy. Natural light lifts our mood, making us more productive, and a view has benefits, too – refocusing on a distant point will help prevent eye strain.

However, a desk should not be located in front of a window, but at right angles to it. This will allow it to be well illuminated without you suffering the eye strain caused by looking directly into light. Natural light can, of course, be moderated through the use of window dressings.

With regards to artificial lighting, a combination of overhead and localized lighting is preferable. An adjustable desk lamp is always useful, and in a confined space a shelf could be fitted above the work surface with a concealed light source on the underside of the shelf.

Test for 'veiled reflection', the glare reflected from computer screens or even from glossy documents, by placing a mirror on your work surface. The 'hot spots' will identify the offending light source, which can be exchanged for light fittings that can manipulate the angle of light. Alternatively, move your desk or your computer.

Storage

Storage in any working environment has to cater for everyday items and also archive material. In the home office, where space is often tight, it is worth making an honest inventory of material you can sensibly archive to store in an attic or storage unit. Remember that you will also need to store paper destined for recycling.

Walls, floors and ceilings

In the spirit of having control over one's environment, pretty much anything goes when it comes to wall, floor and ceiling finishes. However, bear in mind that chair casters will not be kind to fluffy carpets or rugs.

Sound

If you are someone who needs absolute peace and quiet in order to work effectively, and if you have been able to site your home office in a separate room, take the opportunity when redecorating to soundproof the walls, floors and ceilings, as necessary. Soundproofed doors are readily available, as are specialist soundproofing materials (see pages 233–4).

A less technical alternative would be to upholster walls and ceilings or, if space allows, double-line them with plasterboard before decorating. Even something as low-tech as a draught excluder at the base of the door should help keep the sound of the rest of the household at bay.

Music and radio are often welcome accompaniments to work. Consider how best to accommodate this function while preserving your work surface. An extra shelf might do the trick, and ceiling-mounted speakers are unobtrusive.

Meetings

If you need to conduct meetings at your home, you must accept two unavoidable facts:

☐ You will need to accommodate your visitors comfortably, so think about a source of extra seating, and possibly a table. Could you use your dining furniture? Or do you need to make other arrangements, locating extra furniture in your home office?

☐ The access between and including your front door and your designated meeting area, even if this is the kitchen table, should be considered 'home office' territory, and the same careful thought must be applied to the look and function of these areas to preserve professionalism.

Security

You may need to make different security arrangements for your home office to those you would make for your home. Check with your insurance company to make sure you are properly protected in the event of theft or damage.

Treats

The best kind of work does not feel like work. Do not deny yourself treats: a jar of sweets, a basket of fruit, pictures, a comfortable chair or chaise, fresh flowers, music. You, after all, are the boss.

5

finishing off

5

finishing off

If you compare a home to a human body, its finishes, fixtures, furniture and lighting could be described as a wardrobe of clothing and accessories, which can minimize perceived shortcomings and spotlight preferred features in much the same way. You may wish for a bit more 'fullness' in a certain area – but if making a space larger is not an option, then the way you finish and furnish it can make it appear larger. You could call this the 'Wonderbra Strategy'.

MAKING AN INFORMED CHOICE

Choosing objects and materials for the home can be a daunting task, however, when there are so many options and multiple demands from the marketplace to consume. In the end, choice should be informed by the following four criteria:

☐ What you like – that to which you have a positive and personal emotional response, independent of the influence of marketing or the media, or what your friends might be impressed by. You are far less likely to tire of choices made in these circumstances (which is why it is so important to develop confidence in your own unique creativity).
☐ Suitability – what designers call 'fitness for purpose', which should include both short- and long-term performance and durability. Suitability can also involve the idea of practicality, but this is a slightly different idea and can be largely subjective. A finish or fixture may need more care than another to maintain performance but that does not mean it is not practical – it just means you need to do a bit more housework.
☐ Affordability – based not only on available budget but prioritizing that budget, too. It may be worth spending more upfront on less, in the knowledge that the furniture and finishes you do invest in will last much longer than a cheaper equivalent, and so be less expensive in the long run.
☐ Sustainability – a more complicated factor. It involves complex equations that concern the entire life cycle of a product, from raw-material extraction through

to worker welfare and production processes to delivery distances, performance, maintenance and, finally, the potential for recycling.

Sustainability has also become very fashionable, which can sometimes oversimplify matters. The antidote to this is information, which will help protect you from the creeping tyranny of 'green gloss', where hollow claims of environmental and social sustainability are made in order to simply sell more stuff.

Green factors

Whenever you have a product under consideration, ask the supplier not only how a material or fixture performs but also where it is from and how it is made, and then do your research, bearing in mind the following:

☐ The amount of fossil fuel used in the life cycle of a product, from raw material extraction to manufacture and delivery to the store is termed 'embodied energy'. The burning of fossil fuels is blamed for creating climate change and the acidification of our oceans, and consequently changes to our environment. It therefore follows that the less fuel used in the manufacture and delivery of the products we use, the more of a chance we have to minimize their environmental impact.
☐ If you have a concern for resources, then these should not end with delivery. Ask yourself what amount of energy, water, and synthetic or natural ingredients will

be required to maintain or, in the case of electrical fittings, power products.
☐ Chemicals are naturally occurring substances, so be wary of 'green hysteria' concerning their use. While many synthetic chemicals are made from petroleum, these in turn create plastics that can significantly enhance performance and longevity, and make up

Another group of substances to be aware of are endocrine disrupting chemicals (EDCs) such as polybrominated biphenyl (PBB) and polybrominated diphenyl ether (PBDE), which can interfere with our hormones. They are found in brominated fire retardants, commonly used on household textiles such as carpets and upholstered furniture.

☐ Raw-material extraction variously means mining, quarrying, deforestation and animal processing (for example, leather and bone), which can result in habitat destruction, pollution and abuses of animal and worker welfare. Forestry, quarrying and mining in the developed world is usually strictly regulated, but this is not always the case in the developing world. Animal processing can present issues of methane generation, a gas known to contribute to global warming. Animal products used in design and decor are often by-products of the food industry, so any concerns you have over meat and dairy production, and even fisheries, should apply to animal products for the space in which you live.

Once you are armed with this background knowledge, the rule of thumb is to buy things for your home that give you maximum effect with minimum disruption (after asking yourself whether, in this world of abundance, you really need what you think you need in the first place).

the ingredients of many paints, resins and adhesives as well as plastic products. However, not only does their use present the issue of fossil-fuel consumption, but petrochemicals can leach what are called volatile organic compounds (VOCs) that, at best, can irritate – though not everyone is sensitive – and, at worst, are suspected of causing cancer.

As a result of links identified between petroleum-based chemicals and human health, manufacturers are beginning to replace products containing a high level of VOCs with those with low to no VOCs. (However, even something as inoffensive as a lemon can contain VOCs, which are used in the composition of 'organic' paints.)

finishes

Finishes make your home not only look good but also feel good and even smell and sound good. Colour can create atmosphere and manipulate the perception of space through the contrast of dark with pale. Glossy surfaces can amplify space and light through the doubling effect of reflection, while matte or textured surfaces will be invitingly tactile. Sound will reverberate against hard surfaces while soft, pliant surfaces will buffer it. Stone will be cool to the touch where cork is mysteriously warm and silk-velvet is as soft as a kitten's ear. Aromatic timbers such as cedar can fill your home with forest scents, while sisal smells like freshly mown hay.

01

01
Geometrically decorated floor tiles
beautify bath time.

Choosing finishes for our home means we can personalize it on many different sensory levels, and in ways that are both immediately apparent and subliminally seductive. And as long as practical factors are taken into consideration, surfaces can be finished in anything you choose.

A new breed of material libraries that showcase avant-garde finishes can be a revealing resource, though sometimes simply using a conventional finish in a new context can mark your home out from the crowd. For example, the designers Marta Nowicka and Oded Stern designed a real grass lawn as a floor finish for a meeting room. Individualization is only as limited as your imagination, budget and appetite for maintenance.

Having said that, there are also some classic coverings that are worthy of mention. They have become classics because they are tried and tested.

FLOORS

Flooring can constitute the largest single decorative feature in a home, while also having to be high-performing: resistant to the persistent march of feet. So think carefully about this investment.

In certain cases, there may even be fewer flooring options open to you than there are options for wall surfaces. For example, if you were planning a tiled bathroom, you would find that floor tile designs are generally more limited than tiles for walls. This means that you will have more chance of achieving a satisfactory combination if you choose your favourite floor surface before you select a complementary wall finish.

In an open-plan home, variety in floor finishes, and in levels, too, can do the job of walls, delineating zones designed for different activities, while keeping space and light fluid and unobstructed.

Bear in mind that flooring can have an unseen effect on your health. The materials you choose for your flooring can play a significant role in minimizing allergies in those who are sensitive. If you have ever spied whorls of dust rolling across hard floors, like miniature tumbleweed, remember that this 'tumbleweed' is often trapped in a textured flooring such as carpet. Floors can also generate static electricity if they contain artificial substances.

Hard floors can be tough on feet. Pay special attention to this factor in the kitchen, where a hardwearing, easy-to-clean floor is desirable but standing on it for hours while cooking or ironing can take its toll. In wet areas hard floors that are hardwearing can also become dangerously slippery. And then there are those that will be damaged by water.

In homes where young children live, it is worthwhile remembering that little people spend a lot of time on the floor. And they can make a mess. So something that will not hurt them – or be hurt – will be suitable.

Finally, remember that, apart from the front door, floors are the first surface in your home with which you and your visitors will come into contact. You will therefore want your floor to make a good impression.

The rhythm of this parquet flooring is reflected in the shape of the pair of wooden chairs and its patina in the well-used door.

Light coloured parquet flooring lends an otherwise smooth-surfaced space a pleasing texture, with the colour echoed in the shelf and picture frames.

Wide plank flooring, stained white, encapsulates the luxury of simplicity.

Wood

Wood flooring is a perennial favourite, and has been since humans have been building homes. It has all the sensual familiarity of a natural material, and its irregularly patterned character improves with age. Like most natural materials, its character is unique in almost every fragment, so be sure to look at large samples to evaluate variations before committing to an entire floor. A natural character is an animate one, too – wood needs a degree of loving care and attention to get the best out of it, like people.

Wood floors can be used anywhere in the home. Do not listen to those who caution against using it in wet areas, such as bathrooms. Hardwood floors are usually absolutely fine as long as care is taken with installation – applying a water-resistant, flat finish such as oil and wax – and common sense prevails: standing water will warp most things.

The single word 'wood' can be deceptive as there are many variations, and not only

in terms of species. It can be a hardwood or a softwood, though do not be deceived by illustrative syllables – these names are principally botanical. For example, soft-as-marshmallow balsa wood, used in model airplanes, is a hardwood.

For a reliable indication of hardness, which will be relevant to the level of traffic you anticipate, floors can be rated by the Brinell Test, common in Europe, or the Janka Test, the North American equivalent. Ash, a fairly hard wood, is rated at 4.1 on the Brinell Scale (stainless steel gets a rating of 550) and at 1320 on the Janka Scale (balsawood gets a measly 100).

Do not have unrealistic expectations when it comes to wear. All woods, hard or soft, will mark. Personally, I think this adds to their beauty – as a kind of palimpsest. At any rate, nearly all wood floors can be refinished, though the frequency with which you are able to do this depends on the thickness of the wood. To minimize marks, place soft, felt pads

beneath the feet of all furniture. At the thresholds between inside and out, have decent doormats to remove grit from shoes – that is, if you do not designate your home as a shoe-free zone.

Softwoods are generally cheaper than hardwoods because they grow more quickly, and shortcomings in hardness can be offset by compression treatment. Staining can be used to imitate the dark colours of expensive hardwoods, though it is advisable to use stains with low to no levels of VOCs.

Other kinds of floor finish include soap, which needs to be frequently applied but will build a shimmering lustre; lye, a substance that will fix the colour of wood, preventing it from discolouring as it ages (which it will do otherwise); and lacquer or varnish, which, while entirely different substances, tend to be interchangeable terms when it comes to floors and can give a wood floor gloss – though check for VOC levels here, too. But my favourite has to be

an oil and wax finish – which is natural and matte and shows off wood to its best advantage. In addition, it allows for easy patch repair, unlike lacquer or varnish. The texture of a floor can also be manipulated: hand-scraping is one way to accelerate the aging process.

Wood floors need not be finished 'on site', and this can save on mess, disruption and cost. Factory-finished or 'prefinished' boards are common, though sometimes the final effect can verge on the artificial, which runs contrary to the whole point of a natural wood floor.

If you have based your choice on price and performance alone, painting is a good option for less attractive boards. A tip is to paint one colour over another: as the top layer wears, which it inevitably will, the bottom layer is subtly revealed. Paint formulated especially for floors should always be used, as it will be more durable.

In the end the unique selling point of a wood floor is its grain, which is determined by its species and the way the tree was cut. Generally speaking, the closer to the heart of a tree, or the hotter the climate from which it is sourced, the more consistent the grain will be. This is considered the best quality. Wood that is more figured or knotted is the least prized, though in a very simple space the contrast between, say, very 'clean', white walls and very characterful flooring can be appealing.

It really is quite something to remember that every 'ring' in a slice of wood represents a spring season.

Parquet floors, of which there are a variety of well-established formats, end-grain blocks being just one, combine the patterns in wood with patterns in layout. Depending on your patience or budget, the way a wood floor is laid depends entirely upon the effect you are wanting to achieve. Running the boards from the front to the back of a home can exaggerate linear space – though, depending on the structure beneath, it may be necessary to install a subfloor, usually sheets of plywood. In the same vein, boards run on the diagonal can give a space dynamic energy.

A floor made of narrow boards is called strip flooring, whereas wider boards are called planks. Width of board adds another layer to the cake that is choice. Narrow boards are more likely to be in proportion with a smaller space, and wide boards can make slightly larger spaces appear even larger still.

The infinite popularity of wood, though, has put pressure on finite stocks, leading to abuses of natural habitats and human rights. This is why for any wood used you must check it has been certified by a monitoring scheme. FSC (Forestry Stewardship Council) is one of the most reliable, international organizations of this kind, where for every tree felled at least another is planted in its place, contributing to the earth's 'carbon sink'. Wood that is not certified FSC may have been illegally logged.

Pressure on stocks has motivated innovation in wood flooring products – some good, some bad. The principal alternative products are as follows:

- Engineered floors are those in which a varying thickness of the exposed, decorative wood is attached to a cheaper, concealed wood base. The decorative wood is nearly always a more pricey hardwood, though the base can sometimes be made of hardwood, too, albeit a less expensive variety. They are often preferred to solid wood floors, because the engineered wood is more stable and so less likely to warp. This makes them the preferred kind of wood flooring to be fitted over underfloor heating, or over a concrete floor slab, in which a degree of moisture content is unavoidable.

- Laminate wood floors are usually woodfree – a photograph of wood is laminated to a solid base to look like wood flooring – and as a result are very cheap in price, as well as looks. Fake is only convincing if it is clearly meant as a joke. Unfortunately, the melamine resins used to seal this kind of flooring are anything but. And because laminate flooring is not wood, it does not wear like wood, either.

- A cost-competitive alternative to laminate is flooring made up of something such as birch-faced ply sheets, though they do not tend to wear terribly well.

- An alternative to new wood is the reclaimed variety, of which there is a plentiful supply. This will have already been 'broken in' and will have a genuine, rich patina. It may well come with an interesting history, too: the source of reclaimed wood flooring can be surprising.

Whichever kind of wood you choose, it will be only as good as the subfloor underneath. If there is more than a 3mm (1/8in) variation, some kind of levelling treatment will be required – either the application of a self-levelling compound or a ply subfloor (check for VOC levels in the composition in both cases). This must be borne in mind when considering the overall cost in the context of the thickness of the wood floor you select. Do be aware that excavating a ground floor to accommodate a self-levelling compound, plus a thickness of flooring, will be expensive. And significantly shaving off the bottoms of doors or inserting a small, and treacherous, step must be avoided where at all possible.

The cost will also be determined by the type of wood floor product you choose. Most engineered boards are made to lock together to create what is known as a floating floor. This means that engineered boards can be fitted over any kind of existing floor surface – even tile – so long as it is relatively flat. The process is quick, too, and so engineered boards are cheaper to install than glued and nailed solid floors. The downside can be a slightly hollow feeling beneath, which can be offset by the use of a good, thick underlay.

Wood floors should never be 'net fitted' – there should always be a tiny space left around the perimeter of a room, known as an expansion gap, to allow for the wood's reaction to varying degrees of heat and moisture. Your fitter may suggest covering the gap with a thin batten or wood strip, but this will rarely be successful. Ideally, skirtings (baseboards) should be removed, the floor laid and a new skirting fitted over the expansion gap. An alternative is to fit the existing skirting with a slightly shorter 'false' skirting, to create a stepped effect and deliberate detail.

One final note: if you live in an apartment block, maintain harmony amongst your neighbours by fitting substantial insulation beneath your wooden floor. No matter how soft your tread, to them you will sound like a herd of wildebeest in high heels.

01

01

Bamboo is woven to finish walls and floors, where architectural elements, such as the suspended chimney, make the most of the material's lightness and durability.

Bamboo

Bamboo flooring shares many of the properties of wood flooring and compares favourably in terms of price. Like wood flooring, boards can also be supplied as solid or engineered, prefinished or unfinished, and in various widths. Whatever you can do with wood, you can, generally speaking, do with bamboo, too.

The real difference is in sensation. While bamboo can be processed to produce a sufficiently hardwearing floor covering, the feel of the final product retains the lightness, and almost brittle quality, of the bamboo canes you might find at your local garden centre. This can be an appealing characteristic, but to make the most of it all other furnishing elements you add to the room should be similarly 'delicate'. Anything with any kind of mass or density will feel like it is about to crash through the floor.

Bamboo has risen in prominence recently owing to its perceived 'green' credentials, because it grows much more quickly than trees. But do not be seduced by the 'green gloss': it is likely to have travelled a long distance to reach you. And for bamboo there is no scheme comparable to the FSC certification, which means that there is no guarantee of the welfare of workers and their communities. As with wood flooring products, there is also the matter of VOC content in adhesives and factory finishes. Again, knowledge is power, so make enquiries so that you can come to an informed decision.

01
Utilitarian white-painted breeze blocks and cheery modern furniture coalesce on the warm purity of a caramel-coloured cork floor.

02
A smooth white rubber floor, like other elements in this space, is both crisp and comfortable.

Cork

Cork is another natural flooring material that is considered a good substitute for wood. Soft, springy and warm to the touch, cork can feel wonderful underfoot and is an excellent insulator. More sophisticated manufacturing also means it is a lot more wonderful than it was in the 1970s, when no stylish bathroom was complete without a bit of treacle-coloured cork tiling.

Cork flooring now comes not only in square, glue-down tiles but also in engineered boards similar to wood. While colours are typically woody, I have spotted a beautiful and unusual 'whitewashed' version.

Because cork is a renewable and recyclable resource – and can be harvested from the bark of the cork oak (*Quercus suber*) without having to chop down the entire tree – it is highly environmentally sustainable, especially if you live in Spain and Portugal, where most cork oak forests are located. These credentials have been improved upon by more sustainable manufacturing processes. Cork tiles (or boards) are made of granulated cork – the waste from wine bottle cork manufacture – set in resins, which are then pressed. It is now possible to source cork floors that use low-VOC resins and adhesives and that can be finished, and refinished, with natural oil and wax.

Though manufacturers make great claims about cork's durability, I cannot recommend it for high-traffic areas. And while, like wood and bamboo, it is water-resistant, it is not waterproof – so do use it for your bathroom floor but clear up any standing water.

02

Vinyl

Vinyl flooring was developed because it was durable, waterproof and cheaper than natural alternatives. And it still is. It is even beginning to be applied with some attractive surface pattern designs. But its impermeability can cause mould to grow if moisture is trapped beneath. And its durability is its environmental downfall, as vinyl is one plastic that does not biodegrade. Manufacturing processes are also widely reported to be toxic, as is, to some degree, the final product: vinyl (the popular name for PVC, or polyvinylchloride) leaches VOCs.

The pressure to develop new, less toxic and environmentally friendly methods of manufacture – and vinyl products that are easier to recycle as well as biodegradable – has resulted in some impressive innovation in this field that continues to develop. The home decor market will no doubt surely benefit from the results in the future.

Rubber

A natural rubber floor feels fantastic in bare feet, with just enough cushioning. It is durable and waterproof and comes either millpond-smooth or with a stimulating texture, and in a variety of slimline thicknesses. It is the only natural flooring material that is winningly transformed with a drench of colour – and patterns are an option, too. This makes it perfect for children's play areas and bedrooms, not to mention bathrooms and kitchens, where a slightly softer floor will be kinder to hardworking feet. Fitted as tiles or sheets, rubber flooring, like most firm floors, will require a level subfloor.

Rubber, like cork, has become a popular environmentally sustainable choice, because the raw material can be harvested without turning lumberjack. Installation and maintenance using low- to no-VOC adhesives and sealants enhance these 'green' credentials, though some rubber flooring products, both natural and synthetic, may also contain VOC-leaching substances. To be kept looking good and in top condition, rubber floors should be stripped and sealed annually.

Recycled rubber is a more cost-effective alternative to natural rubber and is mostly, if not entirely, synthetic – reclaimed from rubber tyres, which means less waste going to landfill. It can be a bit smelly but, amazingly, it is possible to buy floor deodorant. As is sometimes the case with human bodies, it is debatable which of the two smells might be less offensive.

For seamless purity, especially in open-plan spaces, you might want to consider a poured synthetic rubber floor. Common to commercial and institutional environments, such as factories and hospitals, the absence of seams provides a hygienic environment with good slip-resistance that can be of benefit in the private home. But the biggest benefit is that it looks gorgeous.

Stone, slate and marble

Natural hardness and patterning make stone, slate and marble an enduring choice for floor coverings. And, like wood, stone is a mesmerizing measure of time – the fossilized evidence of prehistory.

Though I have lumped stone, slate and marble together, their characteristics vary enormously. This is the case not only between these three categories but also between different varieties within the categories and even, sometimes, different fragments of each variety from the same quarry. It is therefore wise to inspect a large sample, and, even then, bear in mind that the look of natural materials like these will often be predictably unpredictable. This is why they are loved.

Their porosity varies as much as their looks and makes them vulnerable to stains. Sealing prior to installation with a low- to no-VOC sealant will militate against damage.

Natural patterns can be enhanced with texture. A honed finish gives stone, marble and slate the tempting, matte smoothness of a slice of fudge. 'Tumbling' or 'flaming' are just two ways of achieving the impression of wear; slate can be riven to create the same quality. And the more texture there is, the more the antislip properties.

Edges can be either smooth or rough. Smooth edges will allow for neat, trim, tight joints whereas rough, rustic edges will require deeper grout lines.

Tile sizes and formats vary. Rectangles will always be more dynamic than traditional square shapes, and present more opportunities for being dramatically laid on a diagonal axis.

Whatever you can do to stone, slate or marble outside the home you can do to the same material on floors indoors. I once had a slate floor tile in an entry hall engraved with a line of text.

Weight is often an issue. Always check the strength of your floor structure before you place your order – your supplier or a structural engineer can advise you on this. Check also that the thickness of the material you choose, plus any subfloor, can be comfortably accommodated in your home without having to shave the bottoms of doors.

Stone, slate and marble floors are all excellent heat conductors and can be wonderfully warmed by underfloor heating. Some people find them too cold underfoot without this.

01
A riven slate floor, laid in a classic brickwork pattern, respects the angular form of the contemporary space while contributing to living-room friendly tactility.

02
This polished marble floor adds quiet luxury to an otherwise very simple space.

01
A shiny-shiny resin floor in soft green seamlessly reflects the outside inside in more ways than one.

02
A 'rice-crispie' floor, made of marble chips in resin, forms a stimulating and textured kitchen floor surface.

03
A patchwork of toffee-coloured terrazzo provides a culturally appropriate foundation to a collection of vintage Italian furnishings.

04
A carpet of mosaic tiles cool this conservatory.

Stone 'carpet'

This looks like puffed rice suspended in the palest honey. Made of rounded marble chips and resin, it has a gently knobbly texture promising surreptitious foot massage.

Stone 'carpet' has all the properties of a floor finished in stone tiles or slabs but, because the material is applied by spreading and levelling gobs of it across a floor, it is seamless. The combination of these characteristics makes it a winner for bathroom floors.

Some products may also be refinished. Resins should be checked for VOC content.

Resin floors

Like a stone carpet but without the puffed-rice element, resin floors can give you seamlessness and a light-reflective gloss, similar to poured rubber floors. The difference between the two is that resin is glossier and is available in a wider variety of colours. Scratches can be rubbed out and, when necessary, the entire floor refinished.

Concrete floors

It is easy to assume that concrete floors lend a home a purely industrial aesthetic, but they can be polished to a glamorous, seamless, slip-resistant gloss, the colour of which can be augmented by the addition of pigments or stains. Often chosen for their ability to look like stone, they can be a more affordable option. Concrete behaves like stone, too: concrete floors must be sealed before use and they respond well to underfloor heating. They are also heavy.

'Eco concrete' is an environmentally friendly alternative to standard concrete. It contains a large proportion of fly ash, the waste product from power stations.

Terrazzo

Well-loved terrazzo is like concrete in the sense that it is hard, can be molded, and is another flooring that can be quite heavy. Traditionally made of marble chips suspended in cement and then polished, it has a charming, familiar 'confetti-like' appearance, and its small-scale pattern suits small and large spaces alike.

Terrazzo has always been manufactured from marble waste, but terrazzo products made with other kinds of recycled waste, such as coloured, clear or mirrored glass, in different aggregate sizes, add to your options. These products are all the more attractive as they are more likely to contain low- to no-VOC compounds.

Clay

Floor finishes made of clay range from the toughest porcelain to the roughest brick, and from terracotta and quarry tiles to ceramic and encaustic. All are waterproof, hardwearing and easier to look after than stone, making clay-based materials a favourite for kitchens, bathrooms and entryways.

While some are obviously rustic in appearance and traditional in shape and size, others offer more variety. Porcelain and ceramic tiles can lend colour and consistent texture, and skirtings (baseboards) can be made out of the same material. Varying the shape and size, as well as the colour and pattern, creates multiple opportunities for unique designs.

Hardness varies, too. Porcelain, terracotta, quarry and porcelain tiles are fired at very high temperatures, making them the hardest of all, and suitable for indoor and outdoor applications.

Glazing will moderate gloss but also porosity. Unglazed, matte terracotta tiles should be sealed, as should quarry tiles. The beauty of ceramic and porcelain tiles is that they do not require sealing, are easy to install, are waterproof, will not stain, are easy to maintain, are indestructible under normal conditions and are lightweight.

Tiles can also compensate for imperfections in the subfloor, where the thickness of the adhesive can be adjusted to create a level and smooth final floor. Do not use white grout with flooring tiles, as it will be very difficult to keep that way.

Carpet

Our feet have more than 7,000 nerve endings, so it is not surprising that there is pleasure in sinking feet into the soft pile of a carpet. The sensation was not lost on our ancient forebears: one of the earliest carpets to have been discovered dates from more than 1,500 years ago.

Texture makes carpet an excellent insulator of sound and heat. Its fibrous construction allows for complex patterns, animating spaces that are otherwise plain or adding another alluvial layer of detail to those that are not.

The comforting feel of a carpet, along with its insulating qualities, makes it a perfect choice for bedrooms and other intimate spaces. Carpet has even enjoyed popularity as a bathroom floor finish, though these days such an application is generally considered out of the question; carpet can hardly be described as water-resistant, let alone waterproof. But carpet in the bathroom should not be wholly discounted. If you do not splash when bathing, then carpet can be a nurturing option. It can even be laid over underfloor heating. I cannot recommend carpet in kitchens, however.

Carpets generally have either a woven or a tufted construction. Woven carpet is more expensive because it is of better quality and will last longer. Cord is a type of woven carpet in which the strands are pulled tight to create a ridged effect.

The various types of pile are determined by the way the fibres are treated. Velvet (plush) pile is formally elegant and lush when intensely coloured. Twisted pile is hardwearing, making it perfect for high-traffic areas such as halls. Loop pile has a nubbly texture, while shag pile has sheared, long loops.

Contemporary customized carpet may utilize digital printing or weaving with LED lights. You can also achieve personalization simply by having your carpet layer splice together sections of differently coloured and/or textured carpet. In the same way, some wall-to-wall carpets, especially those in posh hotels, are laid with contrasting borders. The more joins, however, the more the cost.

If you like the idea of having different kinds of carpet in different but adjacent rooms, go ahead. Consistency is for cooking, and 'flow' – that weasel word so beloved of many interior decorators – can often just mean bland.

Carpet originally referred to what we would now call rugs, as in *The Magic Carpet*. Rugs, in turn, can be bought either ready-made or shaped from your favourite carpet with specially bound edges. Ready-made rugs range from the classics such as Occidental Aubussons and Oriental kilims, gabbehs, dhurries and Chinese silk, which will inevitably add exotic spice to a home, to the contemporary.

Rugs are a good option for those who are allergic to dust but still crave a sole-full of softness, whereas carpets are significant dust traps, no matter how much they are vacuumed. Synthetic carpets, while designed to be an affordable but still hardwearing option, may well have been treated with fire-retardant chemicals that will leach, along with other VOCs.

Recycled carpet has joined the ranks of 'eco' products for sale. However, while landfill waste is reduced, synthetic chemical leaching may still be an issue.

The best-quality carpets are woven with natural materials, such as wool, and backed with jute applied with latex adhesive. Unlike synthetic and/or tufted alternatives, they will not 'off-gas' synthetic chemicals. In fact, a pure wool carpet is naturally fire- and soil-retardant.

01

02

Plant fibres

Floor coverings made of plant fibres – coir, sisal, seagrass, tatami and rush – give a floor similar qualities to those of a carpet, such as distinctive texture, and sound and heat insulation. However, they are less likely to trap dust, and so they make a good alternative, free of animal products. Colours are limited to the brown variety, animated by inherent texture. Prized for their natural good looks, these floor coverings can be fitted wall to wall or made into rugs, but should not be used on stairs because they can be slippery.

Some plant-fibre floor materials, such as rush matting, can be distinguished by their nutty, grassy scent, which can be enhanced by weaving in herbs such as rosemary and lavender. Rush mats need moisture, which make them a wonderfully aromatic choice for a bathroom. Outside of a bathroom, they must be frequently 'misted'.

Coir, sisal, seagrass, tatami and rush constitute a kind of United Nations of flora-based carpets. Coir, from the coconut palm, comes mostly from India. Sisal is made from *Agave sisalana*, grown in Brazil and Africa. Seagrass is harvested in China. Genuine tatami is, of course, Japanese, though Scandinavia produces some fine paper-yarn floor textiles. Rush matting is made in the ancient tradition, usually from English water rushes.

The distinctive texture of plant fibres means these coverings can be quite scratchy on little knees, given that small children spend most of their time crawling across floors. However, this can be ameliorated by mixing soft wool into the weave.

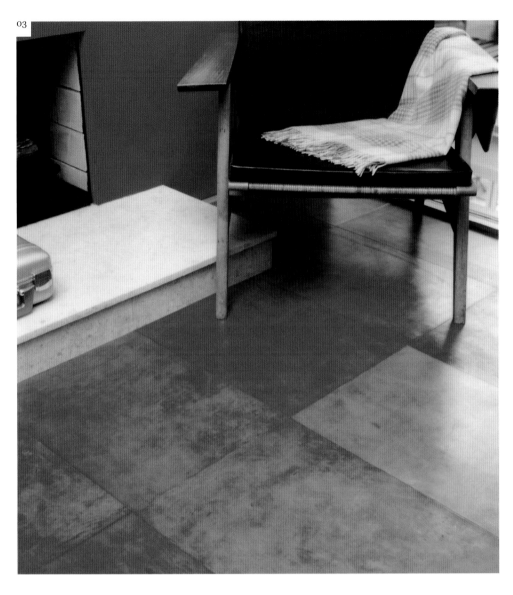

01
A rush mat emphasizes the rustic simplicity of this bedroom.

02
This sisal floor covering demonstrates that it can fit in 'urbane' as well as 'country' surroundings, effortlessly combining here with Modern furniture in a modern space.

03
This tan leather floor will, like a good man, get even better with age.

Linoleum

The most glamorous treatment I have ever seen of humble linoleum was not on a floor but on a wall, in very low light, where I could have sworn it was marble – which neatly illustrates the swan within every ugly duckling. A cheap, hardwearing, waterproof material, linoleum has only come to be thought of as ugly because it has been badly used. Its lovely colours and rich marbling, like Venetian paper, have not been valued as they should. Because it is cheap, its characteristics have been tolerated rather than loved.

Interest in natural materials has prompted a renaissance in linoleum, which is made chiefly from linseed oil, hence the first syllable in the name. As a result of this newfound popularity, not only are the traditional marbled patterns available but it now also comes with a crocodile-effect texture, as well as in a limited range of solid colours.

Leather

For lavish luxury, floors finished in leather are hard to beat. Nor are they cheap. But you will know from the leather shoes you wear how this material is hardworking, is water-resistant and can burnish beautifully with use. Leather floors can be coloured, stitched and tooled in the same way as any other leather product. In a home, they will insulate against sound and heat loss, too.

But the fact remains that leather production can be a noxious process. Industrialized cattle ranching, in countries such as Brazil, can necessitate deforestation to feed the global demand for leather, as well as meat and dairy products. (Cattle raised on such a huge scale also produce considerable amounts of globe-warming methane.) And the environmental and child-labour abuses of unregulated tanneries in countries such as India are real cause for alarm.

It is therefore reassuring to know that tanneries in most developed nations are subject to strict environmental controls and that an increasing number of suppliers are distinguishing themselves by the supply of organic leather from organic cows dyed using vegetable dyes. The same concerns, and investigations as to sustainable provenance and processing, should be applied to the use of other kinds of hides and skins.

WALLS

Wall finishes, like those for floors, can protect the inner fabric of your home and characterize its atmosphere on many sensory levels. Specifically, wall finishes can manipulate perspective, as they are immediately detectable at eye level. This means that your choice of wall finish may be your most powerful weapon against spaces you feel to be too small or not cosy and intimate enough.

As with floors, the choice of finish is entirely personal, and though practicalities should be heeded your choice need not be restricted by convention. Having said that, here are some tried and tested options that are worthy of study and, in some cases, complete re-evaluation.

01
Horizontal bands of blue/green paint colour individualize this bedroom and are perfectly complemented by warm timber tones, snowy whites, a bright blue and a leaf green, the whole concentrated in a well-chosen landscape painting.

Paint

The most accessible form of wall finish, paint is also the cheapest. The supply is abundant, it is easy to apply and it comes in a million different colours, shades and tones, not to mention numerous finishes and a range of textures. It can be used anywhere, from wet bathrooms to drier living rooms.

Paints come in various finishes – from matte or satin to eggshell or gloss – that will each create different interior effects. Special moisture- and steam-resistant paints are also available that have been specially formulated for wet and steamy environments such as bathrooms and wet rooms.

Because it turns walls into an artist's canvas, paint has the potential for infinite creative personal expression. It is also the most imitative form of wall finish: a paint effect can suggest anything from marble to wood. Murals, or trompe l'oeil (meaning 'trick the eye'), can even suggest a world beyond, both figuratively and spiritually.

Painting architectural details in a colour, shade or tone that contrasts with the main wall colour will serve to highlight those details. (There is no law, by the way, that prohibits the painting of woodwork in something other than white gloss.) Paint can even imitate architectural details that simply do not exist. Another way to play tricks is to use fluorescent paint, which is perceptible only in the dark.

With such enormous scope, experimentation is essential. It is also perfectly realistic, given the very affordable price of a pot of paint and the ease of application. If you are nervous about developing your ideas directly on your walls, try them out on large sheets of paper or card (posterboard), which can be taped to your walls. Study the effect throughout the day and also at night, because it will change. Remember that a wall can easily be repainted, so this is the place to take a risk.

Colour is one way of defining paint choice; application is another, and there is also the matter of ingredients. Paint can contain synthetic petroleum-based chemicals that leach VOCs. As our awareness of environmental health is raised, paints have been developed in which VOC levels are either low or absent. (However, natural VOCs, such as those found in a lemon or in turpentine, are often used in what are marketed as 'organic' paints – very few paints will, in truth, be VOC-free.)

Perhaps the purest of the pure are paints made of milk or water and coloured with naturally occurring pigments. These are the paints our forebears used, such as limewash, casein paint, clay paint and distemper (calcimine). These traditional paints are also distinguished by their permeable qualities, making them especially suitable for similarly traditional buildings that lack a dampcourse – if damp can come inside, it needs to find a way out, too.

Interest in less toxic paint has helped to drive the popularity of historical or 'heritage' paint colour palettes. This is a perhaps welcome reaction to the hegemony of faux paint effects of the 1980s, when you could barely move without the risk of being rag-rolled.

The use of logic deftly avoids the decorative tyranny of the feature wall: the candy-striped wallpaper chosen reinforces architectural lines, and its pattern and colour resonate in the shiny lime-green panel, too.

Wallpaper

Unless you have lived like a hermit for the last decade, you will know that wallpaper has enjoyed a florid renaissance and as a result the market is full of stimulating designs. Pattern can inform not only decorative style but spatial perception, too: open patterns on light backgrounds will suggest depth, while dense or dark patterns will 'cosy up' a room; papers with an open vertical motif will visually raise a ceiling, while those with an open horizontal motif will lend breadth.

Textured wallpapers can add voluptuous tactility, and some of my favourites include hessian (burlap), silk, grasscloth, embroidered wallcoverings and certain flocked varieties. It is even possible to buy magnetic wallpaper. Developments in printing technology have created 'interactive' wallpapers where the play of light will vary perception. But, of course, the more elaborate the design and technique, the more expensive it will be.

If you have heard about the renaissance in wallpaper you will also have heard about 'feature walls', where a single wall is finished with a wallpaper or paint to contrast with adjacent walls. The ubiquity of this idea, not least on home makeover television shows, where limited budgets must still produce 'big' effects, has devalued it, and 'feature walls' now look like an over-cautious dip into home decorating. If you are going to wallpaper, do so with conviction, either over all walls or partially on all walls, for example below or above a chair rail. And remember, wallpaper borders are rarely chic.

Wallpaper can be applied to any room, even moist areas like kitchens and bathrooms. However, specialist applications like this usually necessitate the use of VOC-containing vinyl.

It is often thought that wallpaper can hide a multitude of sins, but it can highlight imperfections if the walls are not properly prepared. The cost of wallpaper depends on the wallpaper you choose plus the state of the walls for which it is destined.

The least environmentally harmful wallpapers are those printed on paper from managed forests, for example those certified by the Forestry Stewardship Council (FSC), and printed with water-based inks. They should then be pasted with an adhesive that is acrylic- and solvent-free, and free of fungicides, preservatives and synthetic resins.

02

02
An intriguing application of wallpaper beneath a notional chair rail that gives depth to this black, white and brown scheme.

03
A peacock feather motif lends a sense of perspective, and the indigo blue and white are perfectly balanced by the colour of rust.

04
Woodland creatures at home.

03

04

Ceramic and glass tiles

Ceramic and glass tiles, including mosaics, are thought of as a suitable wall finish only for bathrooms and kitchens, but this is because they are hardwearing and waterproof. For these very reasons they would also be an appropriate application in an entry hall, especially as ceramic tile has recently become more decorative. Retro style is influencing contemporary designs, which could justify use in other spaces, too.

The decorative quality of ceramic and glass tile is not solely determined by its size, colour, texture or pattern. The way it is laid, in terms of direction and joint size, and the colour of the grout add to the final effect. Minimal, narrow joints make for a very neat, clean look, while wider joints add to overall detail. Tiles laid on the diagonal will give a space dynamism. And grout is available in many different colours, even bright ones, which can look impressive.

Square formats have, until recently, been the convention but more interesting shapes, including ovals and octagons, are becoming more popular. And digital printing means that tiles printed with your own designs are well within reach, though obviously not the cheapest choice. If you would like to use a very expensive type of tile but are on a limited budget, the 'a little goes a long way' strategy must be deployed, where just a small amount can be used to contrast with something more affordable.

The wall surface for which your tile is destined needs to be reasonably flat. However, tile adhesive is designed to compensate for differences in level and is available with low to no VOCs.

The manufacturing of tiles is sometimes considered to have a high 'embodied energy' coefficient, as tiles need to be fired. But production waste is often recycled, and tiles, as we know from ancient Roman mosaics, can last a very long time.

02

01
Patterned tiles form a gloriously
wild backdrop to an otherwise
perfunctory kitchen.

02
A wall of painted 'concrete eggs'
in the exquisite Hotel Parco dei
Principi on Italy's Amalfi coast,
designed by Gio Ponti.

03
Lustrous plaster forms a
waterproof splashback in
this bathroom, and handy
recesses, too.

03

Polished plaster

Having originated in Italy and having the
ability to look like marble, polished plaster
is also known as Venetian, Italian or marble
plaster. Apart from a marble finish it can
also be made to look like other kinds of
natural stone or even suede. Alternatively,
it can be simply coloured.

With the added benefit of being
waterproof, polished plaster is suitable
even in showers. It is also considered
environmentally friendly because it
contains all natural ingredients.

Walling

The professional technique of upholstering
walls with softly padded fabric, walling
irresistibly tailors a room. Not only does it
feel luxurious, but it also insulates against
sound and, especially, cold, hence its
popularity in old country houses. Of course,
the choice of fabric determines the look, much
like wallpaper. Variation can be achieved
with stitching and edge-tape details.

Walling is not suitable for the entire
height of a wall, however. The lower section,
up to around hip level, should always be
faced with something harder, to protect this
typically high-contact section. It also serves
as a pleasingly sharp contrast to the more
yielding upholstery above.

Obviously walling is not suitable for
kitchens and bathrooms, but it will be
fabulous in any other part of your home.
Though not an inexpensive option, it is
worth every penny.

Panels of antiqued mirror on the
walls amplify volumes of space
with discreet elegance.

A wall finished in external-grade
unpainted chipboard successfully
subverts conventions.

Mirrored and coloured glass

Another favourite wall treatment of mine
is mirroring, where the visual trick of
doubling the amount of space and light
available still tickles me, especially when
mirrors are mounted opposite each other to
create an infinite series of spaces. This kind
of magic means that you do not need a great
deal of mirror to create a great deal of effect:
the mirrored rear surface of even a small
recess will give the impression of there being
as much space as there is reflected, which
can be a lot. In the same vein, you might even
want to try horizontal or vertical slivers of
mirror on a wall, which will give the effect
of just a glimpse into a space beyond.

Mirrors come in lovely colours and
finishes, and the imperfections of genuine
antique mirrored glass are beguiling.
Coloured mirrors include those in grey,
green, peach, blue and gold. Other
decorative finishes are usually of
the artificially antiqued kind, though
mirrors can be printed and engraved, too.

Sheets of glass will reflect space
and light in the same way as mirrored
glass, but more subtly. They can be
coloured in as many colours as there
are paints – the darker the colour, the
more the depth of reflection. Just be
sure to ask for 'low iron' glass, which
will remove the green tinge that is
detectable in all standard glass and
that could otherwise compete with your
chosen colour.

With its large, toughened, waterproof
sheets that minimize bacteria-trapping
joins, this form of alluring, glossy colour
is ideal for bathrooms and kitchen
splashbacks. It is especially good for
small bathrooms and kitchens, which
will benefit from the impression of extra
light and space.

Both mirrored and coloured glass can
be mounted on all reasonably flat surfaces
using a low-VOC adhesive. And all glass
can be recycled.

03
Panels with a distinctive timber
veneer are an appealing contrast
to the black gloss on the chest
of drawers.

Wood

Wood panelling makes a wall tough, can hide a multitude of sins and can animate, too, giving depth and a lively finish. It is extremely versatile and can even be used in bathrooms, though I would not recommend it for areas that will be directly hit by water, unless it is made from a sustainable tropical hardwood.

Traditional formats include the familiar fielded panelling, which presents a grid of raised planes. To distort perspective, twist crosspieces away from the vertical and horizontal axes, playfully modernizing this technique.

Fielded panelling can be stained and treated to look like more expensive timber or like a completely different material, such as marble. However, such theatre is often best left to theatre designers, honesty of materials being an indicator of good design.

Fielded panelling is also popular in a painted finish, as is tongue-and-groove, both creating the easy comfort of a familiar, traditional look. Modern wood panelling with simpler detail is common in Modernist homes, where hardwood grains are oiled to a dark, amber lustre.

For a more subversive feel, boards in an engineered wood product usually used in construction, such as plywood, chipboard (particleboard) or OSB (oriented strand board) can be used. It is now possible to source these boards with low-VOC resins and adhesives.

The use of any type of wood panelling should be subject to the same kind of environmental scrutiny as the use of any other wood product.

01

03

02

01
Heavily aggregated concrete
is leavened with smooth-
surfaced furnishings.

02
The ever-developing, rusted
appearance of metal tiles
animate this shower cubicle.

03
Concrete is served up as smoky-
grey panels – a waterproof wall
finish appropriate to a bathing area.

Engineered stone

This offers the hardness of stone with the colour consistency and waterproof character of plastic, making it perfect for bathrooms and kitchens. It is principally made up of quartz, a finite natural resource, set in petroleum-based resins. Manufacturers have begun to offer low-VOC engineered stone products, with enhanced characteristic durability and impermeability. They come in a range of seductive stone-inspired and brighter shades and colours.

Plastic composites

Also known as solid surfacing, sheets of plastic composite such as Corian or LG Hi-Macs make walls shatterproof, waterproof and highly coloured with minimal joins, so they are a good choice for bathroom walls and even showers. They are also much lighter than the glass or stone equivalents, which may be relevant depending on the state of your walls, or the weight tolerance of your floors.

A more 'environmentally friendly' alternative would be sheets of recycled plastics, their attractive swirling patterns creating an almost marbled effect. While composites such as Corian can be imperceptibly joined together, their recycled equivalent demands a clear and purposeful edge-to-edge detail, such as a small bevel, or the join will look untidy.

Metal

Metal might not sound like a very inviting wall covering for a home, but rusted metal panels, or reclaimed matte steel, the colour of lead, can add not just indestructible durability but a sculptural aesthetic, too, especially in large, ex-industrial living spaces. Even reclaimed, printed metal advertising hoardings could be considered as an eccentric and often inexpensive wall finish.

Laminates

A laminate material is one that is designed to be glued to another stronger core. A well-known example is Formica, which can be laminated to a smooth-surfaced wood composite like plywood. Recently transformed from 'caff' naff to designer delight, Formica is available in myriad colours, textures and patterns, including those you can design yourself.

In a sense, you could construe laminate as a wallpaper, partly because paper makes up a majority of the ingredients, alongside plastic. It offers all the pattern and texture that wallpaper can offer, but is even more durable, which make it a rather good material for a splashback. It is also temptingly affordable.

Laminated panels will need to be made up by a carpenter, who will probably also need to laminate the concealed rear, in order to prevent warping. This is called 'counterbalancing'.

Concrete

You may be surprised to discover that concrete can make for a decorative wall finish, but the innovative British design company Concrete Blond has harnessed concrete's sculptural qualities to produce 'three-dimensional' wallpapers, where unfashionable vinyl papers lend their unloved texture to urban concrete to create an excitingly subversive, and indestructible, waterproof wall finish. They are now made in very lightweight panels so, unusually for concrete, loading is not an issue.

Leather

Leather can give a wall natural protection and an evolving patina. For more detail see the information about leather floors on page 183.

Stone, slate and marble

To clad walls in stone, slate or marble,
you will need strong walls as well as a
strong wallet. If it is within your means,
the investment will be worthwhile in
bathrooms and the kitchen, which will
benefit from the characteristic durability
and impermeability, at least when
properly sealed. Richly veined marbles
are particularly beautiful.

Another kind of stone finish is fieldstone,
in which uncut stones form both structure
and final finish. The effect is typical of
traditional rustic homes and resurgent in
Modernist architecture.

Brick

Exposed brick walls only suit certain
environments, either the vernacular or
where there is a decisive contrast between
the raw qualities of brick and rather more
crisp surroundings.

Ceilings

In grand homes through history, ceiling
decoration has been an elaborate affair,
a confection of mouldings and carvings,
paint and gilt. Such indulgent treatment
was palely imitated in more modest homes,
a good example being the plaster mouldings
you might find in a Victorian town house.

Modern times have ignored the
decorative potential of ceilings, and the
usual treatment is a coat of white paint,
because this will reflect the most light
back into a room. But so will pale colours:
a paler tone of the colour on your walls
will always work well and be just that bit
more individual.

You could even be more adventurous.
Bear in mind that any colour that is the
tiniest shade darker than your walls will
give the impression of reducing the height
of a space – this may be desirable in a room
where the ceiling feels uncomfortably high.

fixtures

Fixtures are those objects in your home that are fixed in place. For this reason it is worth taking more care over their selection than for less permanent items. Effectiveness can be difficult to evaluate without first testing, but this is not always realistic. Instead, think carefully about the purpose of the fixtures – what designers call 'functionality'. Be sure to ask suppliers as many questions as you feel relevant – this is what good suppliers expect.

Kitchen cabinets

A built-in, or fitted, kitchen can make the most of available space. Because storage is compartmentalized into a series of drawers, cupboards, shelves and open recesses, you can find what you need when you need it.

Built-in kitchens are manufactured in a number of different ways and in different materials. The adage 'pay cheap, pay twice' could not be more appropriate.

In the best type of cabinet the carcass – a rather cadaverous word for the interior of a cabinet – is made of marine-grade ply in a solid wood frame. The ply, unlike solid wood, is resistant to the kind of moisture typically found in a kitchen and so will not warp. The solid wood frame gives the cabinet strength, while traditional joining techniques, such as biscuit joints, increase strength even more.

The next grade down consists of cabinet carcasses made of MDF (medium-density fibreboard), which will expand if wet. Last, and least, are carcasses made of melamine-faced chipboard (particleboard).

This material looks like breakfast cereal and behaves in much the same way.

In the case of semi-customized and what might be called 'stock' kitchens – where what you see is what you get – overall quality is also indicated by the types of drawer runners and hinges used. The best drawer runners are metal, based on a ball-bearing mechanism. The least reliable are plastic. Hinges should be adjustable, as should internal shelves. The best closures are 'soft close', where drawers and doors have special fittings that stop them from banging shut.

The lower cabinets, or base units, will usually be mounted on adjustable legs. These are essential for a level countertop, to avoid cracking and things rolling off it. These legs are masked by a kick plate. In very small kitchens additional drawers can be fitted here.

The best wood cabinet doors are made of unglued solid timber, while the best pretenders will be veneered with a good, solid wooden edge. Glossy finishes, such as a spray finish, will amplify light and space and can add a bit of spicy colour. They will also take a bit more care and effort to keep glossy.

Steel will be indestructible but noisy. Plastic laminate is an affordable alternative to consider, and newly sophisticated designs in alluring colours and patterns make it an attractive alternative.

Glass doors, especially if they are internally illuminated, not only add visual interest to a run of cabinet doors, but also help visually to 'stretch out' a small kitchen, as well as contributing another ambient light source. Sliding doors are convenient in a restricted space.

Given the amount of activity in a kitchen, the practicalities of access and use are fundamental. As a result, drawers for pots and pans, crockery and glassware have become popular – no more throwing yourself into the back of a cupboard in search of that elusive pot. For the same reasons it is now possible to buy refrigerators and dishwashers contained in drawers.

Visually, a built-in kitchen can be distilled into a series of architectural lines – the vertical and the horizontal. These lines can make or break the look, and broken lines break the look even more. This is why appliances will look better if integrated – and why a run of wall cabinets interrupted by a non-integrated extractor fan often looks clumsy.

The balance between the lines of vertical cupboards and horizontal drawers is also a determining factor. Cabinets that conceal a set of drawers can maintain purely vertical lines, but a rather rigid specification like this is entirely a matter of personal taste.

If you are an extreme purist you may want to consider cabinets that can contain small appliances such as toasters and kettles, which can then be hidden behind pocket doors, or tambours, when they are not in use.

Standard lower cabinets are normally 900mm (35$\frac{1}{2}$in) high by 600mm (24in) deep and of varying widths, such as 300mm (12in), 400mm (15$\frac{3}{4}$in), 500mm (19$\frac{3}{4}$in), 800mm (31$\frac{1}{2}$in) and 1000mm (39$\frac{1}{2}$in). Then there are full-height cabinets, often called 'pantry' or 'larder cabinets', and those that are three-quarter height, giving maximum storage within easy reach.

When selecting your kitchen, think about the quality of line and also mass and proportion. You will find that shorter, wall-mounted cabinets are always in pleasing proportion to the accompanying base units. But if you want taller upper cabinets, the ones that reach to the ceiling, so long as they are minimally detailed, will be in better balance with the lower cabinets than anything in between. Whatever their height, wall cabinets will usually be a standard 300mm (12in) depth, so that you avoid knocking your head while working at a countertop.

One visual trick, which will counteract any sense of heaviness in a run of lower cabinets, is to face the kick plate with mirrored steel. Not only will it be tough,

01

but it will also give the impression that your cabinets are floating. Another way to achieve this effect is to conceal a lighting strip along the length of the kick plate. These ideas will be possible so long as cabinets do not integrate appliances that require venting at the base.

The fronts of doors and drawers can be made of or finished in any rigid, wipe-clean material your imagination allows. And changing fronts is one cost-effective, not to mention environmentally sensitive, way of giving yourself what will feel like a whole new kitchen. Any wood products used in fitted kitchens should be FSC-certified and contain low to no VOCs.

Hardware – handles and knobs – can be the jewel on the dress that is the kitchen, completing an outfit or distracting attention from it, as necessary. In a minimalist kitchen the most minimal handles will be integrated and invisible. Slimline contemporary designs usually come as bars – again, pay attention to lines and the mix of horizontal and vertical. Truly jewel-like hardware, such as that made of coloured glass, can prettily ornament a plain kitchen.

Bathroom storage
Bathroom storage includes wall-mounted, often mirrored cabinets such as medicine cabinets, and floor-mounted vanity units. Given the abundant presence of water in this room, the same concerns apply here about materials as for kitchen cabinets (see page 197).

Splashbacks and countertops

Whether in a kitchen or bathroom, using the same material for both the splashback and the countertop looks slick, especially if the splashback is run tight into the underside of any overhead cabinet. Glossy materials, such as coloured glass, will play interesting tricks with light and space, but beware of reflecting not-so-attractive concealed under-cabinet light fixtures. In this case the lights should be hidden behind a smart diffusing panel.

Countertops need to be hardwearing and water-resistant. In the kitchen it is useful for them also to be heat-resistant, but trivets will provide additional protection from hot pans. Similarly, the assiduous use of chopping boards will help prevent damage from sharp knives in the kitchen.

Seamless countertops are the most hygienic. These can be made of composite materials like plastic composite, concrete or engineered stone, including the new generation of terrazzo-type materials containing recycled glass and sometimes other ingredients, such as seashells. However, these materials will not necessarily be completely seam-free. This is because the fabrication of countertop materials is limited by on-site construction systems or, if made off-site (away from your home), the access around any corners between the street and your kitchen.

01
The plastic qualities of engineered stone are brought to bear on a smooth and seamless countertop and its up-stand.

02
A mirrored splashback is a glamorous addition to a no-nonsense commercial kitchen-style countertop.

03
The well-proven durability of
reclaimed timber makes for a
predictably sound countertop.

04
A lava stone countertop in mustard
yellow performs and prettifies,
while the gleaming stainless-steel
splashback echoes the sink and
taps (faucets).

Sheet materials that could be used include the following:

- Glass, which will look like a lovely layer of fruit jelly.
- Pyrolave, an eyewateringly expensive enamelled volcanic stone that comes in zingy colours.
- Plastic laminate, which is perhaps the least hardwearing, though it still performs well, comes in a variety of colours and patterns, and is improved by a good, solid edge.
- Stainless steel, which is used in professional kitchens and which after years of use will develop an accretion of little scratches.
- Zinc, the favourite of French bars, which will also develop a pleasing patina.

Then there are the natural favourites: wood and stone. Wood for countertops and splashbacks needs to be a type of hardwood and should be FSC-certified or reclaimed. Stone, whether it is marble, granite, slate or limestone, will always need to be sealed. Stone that has been honed – polished to a matte finish – will look subtle and sophisticated, though a bit of reflective gloss may be helpful in a small or dark space.

Granite's remarkable hardness makes it a common choice for countertops in kitchens, but therein lies its downfall. The pink variety looks like sausage meat, but there are some more unusual granites available in white or palest green, which would be a much more individual choice.

A tiled countertop and splashback can look good, especially when uneven, handmade tiles are used. However, it will need to be frequently bleached to keep the grout clean.

The look of a countertop is also affected by its edge detail. Thinner countertops can be made to look more luxurious by applying a thicker edge piece. Edges are sometimes riven to add character, though beware as this detail can become a bug trap.

An alluring splashback effect is where translucent materials – such as acrylic-type panels, which are now available in recycled 'eco resins' and set with confections of things like real grass – are illuminated from the rear. This will serve to 'dematerialize' what is behind – useful in smaller kitchens or bathrooms – and add another ambient lighting effect.

The issue of hygiene has been exploited by manufacturers of some countertop and splashback materials, marketing the addition of antimicrobial treatments as a unique selling point. However, many antimicrobial treatments use a chemical called triclosan or triclocarban that is 'bioaccumulative'. This means that it takes far longer to be excreted from an organism than it does to be ingested, which is a problem, as these chemicals are suspected of being toxic or even carcinogenic. And in the end, studies have shown that in ordinary circumstances good old-fashioned soap and water is just as capable of killing germs as antimicrobial treatments. *In extremis*, as in other situations, alcohol is also effective.

Brassware

Brassware refers to taps (faucets), shower heads and wastes. It comes in different styles and more finishes than just brass. For a matte metal finish, choose brushed steel, chrome or nickel, which always looks best in traditional surroundings. Matte brass can be lovely, too, though near impossible to source in anything other than salvage yards. For a shiny finish, choose chrome. Some manufacturers even offer juicy fruit colours.

Taps – whether for kitchen or bathroom sinks or baths – can be 'deck-mounted' (mounted on the horizontal plain) or wall-mounted. In some countries, the suitability of certain tap designs is affected by water pressure, so it may be worth checking your water pressure before making an investment. Your water authority or a plumber will be able to advise.

Three-hole mixers consist of separate hot and cold taps plus a single mixer spout (spigot). Monobloc taps (single-lever faucets) are single-spouted and levered, mixing hot and cold water. Pillar taps are the traditional kind, where hot water comes out of the hot tap and cold water out of the cold tap. A swan-neck spout looks like a swan's neck.

In the kitchen I prefer to have taps that can be turned on with my elbow when my hands are encrusted in pastry. In some of the kitchens that I have designed, I have specified hospital taps with extra-long 'arms' designed for just this purpose.

Kitchen taps have recently undergone a wave of innovation. Fittings are now widely available that can dispense filtered water and others that provide constant boiling water. Phallic spray attachments are also available, though you would need to be rinsing restaurant quantities of pots and vegetables to justify one of these rather conspicuous behemoths. There are also kitchen and bathroom taps that can illuminate – red for hot, blue for cold – which I suppose obviates the need for the 'H' and 'C'.

The waste – that is, the drain and plug in the sink, and sometimes the plumbing below – should be chosen to match the taps. In a bathroom where the sink is wall-mounted and the plumbing exposed, a 'bottle trap' waste will make the plumbing look decorative. As well as the familiar old-fashioned plug on the end of a chain, wastes can be pop-up, flip-up or push-up/down.

The most flamboyant shower heads are 'rain showers', which aspire to emulate the effect of rain. The heads are usually large and square and can use an awful lot of water, but aerating water and fitting a flow regulator can help to maximize effect without being greedy. This applies to taps as well.

A shower can be integrated (where the controls and the head are visible but none of the connecting pipework) or surface-mounted. A thermostatic control is always

01
Conventional copper piping and valves make an unconventional bathroom mixer tap.

02
Brushed-chrome pipes and the kind of valves that are usually concealed, combine to create an interesting focal point.

03
A simple, contemporary kitchen mixer is matched with a popular pan washer.

04
A perfectly machined kitchen countertop invisibly integrates sink and drainer, where simplicity and practicality are echoed in the design of the mixer tap and the sculptural bowl.

04

an advisable protection against scalding. Some shower valves allow you to control both temperature and flow. Taps with ceramic disc valves will resist debris and limescale.

Baths can be filled without taps. Exafill fittings double as tap and bath waste, which is ideal in very minimal bathrooms. Freestanding baths can also be served by tall, floor-mounted taps.

Sanitaryware
This is the antiseptic term for those 'vessels' peculiar to kitchens and bathrooms: kitchen and bathroom sinks, bathtubs, shower trays, shower stalls, toilets and bidets.

Kitchen sinks
The best kitchen sinks are big. A popular configuration is one and a half sinks – one large, one much smaller, perhaps fitted with a waste-disposal unit – so that when the larger one is in action, the smaller one can deal with draining or rinsing things.

Kitchen sinks can be made of an array of materials that range from serviceable stainless steel to highly decorative beaten copper, vitreous china or stone. The sleek choice is integrated sinks, which are made out of the same material as the adjacent countertop (and where the countertop usually has grooves carved into it for drainage).

Sinks that are not integrated can be inset (offered into the countertop from above) or undermounted (bonded to the underside of the countertop), which is much more chic and more practical, as a rim of an inset sink can often trap dirt. Belfast (apron) sinks are large, deep, rectangular sinks that are usually ceramic. They require a section of the countertop to be removed from the front to the rear, as opposed to a cutout.

01
A carefree mix of luxury and
modesty is manifest in this
bathroom, where an opulent (and
very heavy) marble bath sits in
front of a painting-cum-splashback,
both accompanied by a simple side
table for bathing accessories.

02
A galvanized steel tub, balanced
on wooden beams, performs as
bath and shower in the raw.

Baths

Much of the sanitaryware in bathrooms
is made of vitreous china – apart from
the bath. Baths were originally made of
cast iron, which is still possible to source,
though mainly from reclamation yards.
Enamelled steel is a slightly lighter
alternative. Acrylic and a plastic known as
ABS (acrylonitrile-butadiene-styrene) are
lighter still. Sometimes, though, unbearable
lightness can be applied as much to baths as
it can to being: ABS is cheap and flimsy and
will turn yellow in ultraviolet light.

The quality of acrylic baths, on the other
hand, has improved exponentially over
recent years. Its advantage over enamelled
steel is that any scratches can be polished
out, whereas superficial damage to enamel
requires re-enamelling – though this is
easy enough for any professional to do
and can be done on site. However, the use
of acrylic in sanitaryware raises the usual
environmental issues when it comes to
plastics. A bath, like a kitchen sink, can
be either undermounted or inset into
surrounding panelling. Or it can be
freestanding, particularly if it deserves to
be centre stage because it is a nice shape,
is made of a fine material such as marble
or copper, or even has been formed on site
out of something like concrete. Japanese-
inspired wood and stone composites are
equally luxurious alternatives.

01

Shower trays

In terms of the choice of material, shower trays are not dissimilar to baths, ranging from acrylic to marble, and also including vitreous china. If you have the available floor depth, the most elegant shower trays are those that can be recessed so that they are flush with the floor. Be aware that acrylic trays can be prone to slight movement.

Shower stalls

The most elegant shower stalls are those constructed out of large panes of glass, fitted with a frameless glass shower door. A less expensive shower door option is one that is fitted into a metal frame. Glass used in shower stalls can be treated to help prevent a build-up of limescale.

Avoid at all costs those shower stalls that look like a version of the flight deck of the *Starship Enterprise*, stuffed with integrated jets and probably an espresso maker. These things are just ludicrous.

01
Engineered stone moulds itself into
a one-of-a-kind bathroom basin.

02
This ceramic hand-wash basin is
prettily sweet.

toilets can be either entirely wall-hung (and are likely to be fitted to a concealed metal brace) or back to the wall. Nevertheless, concealed cisterns may not always be an option, in which case the modern alternative is a close-coupled toilet. The flush should be of the dual variety to conserve water.

Toilets come with many add-ons these days, from a carwash effect, which rinses and dries, to a heated seat, while the benefit of these features is a matter of very personal preference. What can be useful is a soft-close seat, which will not clatter or trap children's fingers when lowered.

Bidets

If you have a bidet it should match the toilet, as they will be adjacent and any difference in colour or style would be immediately apparent.

The colour of sanitaryware is most often white, but colour is back – and pattern, too, though this is admittedly somewhat avant-garde, which usually means pricey. For more affordable colour fun, try salvage yards: there are companies who specialize in vintage coloured sanitaryware. It is wholly acceptable to mix white sanitaryware from different suppliers, so long as there is enough distance between the items so that any slight variations in colour will not be noticeable.

Bathroom sinks

Bathroom sinks are available in a variety of designs. On a pedestal sink the plumbing is concealed by a matching column beneath. A vanity sink is fitted into the vanity unit beneath, to conceal plumbing and provide storage. A sit-on vessel sink sits like a bowl on a surface such as a countertop. A wall-hung sink, with chrome bottle trap, will always add contemporary clarity, and be easy to clean underneath, but the plumbing is visible.

A vessel sink, which looks like a bowl, can be a nice touch for hand washing alone: anything more and it will feel very restrictive, and the surface it sits on can get very wet after use. Glass bowl basins will be a devil to keep shiny, too. To know whether a sink will 'fit' you or not, hold your hands to your face, as if washing, and note how far apart your elbows are, as this is the point to which water will drip and eventually from where it will fall.

Toilets

Toilets were originally designed with high-level cisterns (tanks), and subsequently with low-level cisterns. Now the fashion is completely concealed cisterns, which is my personal favourite. Concealed-cistern

Doors

When choosing objects and finishes for the home, it is all too easy to overlook practicalities in favour of good looks, but the opposite is true with doors. A door has as much potential to make a decorative and even spatial contribution as any other surface or object. While usually chosen to suit the period or style of a home, a door can be treated as a blank canvas in much the same way as a wall, and painted or patterned to suit.

Installing taller than standard doors is a designer's trick, to give the impression of more height than there actually is in a space. Doors the same height as walls will reduce the number of perceptible lines and are therefore suitable for a minimalist approach.

Hardware

Door 'furniture', also known as ironmongery, includes those items, mostly made of metal, that give added functionality to your doors and windows. They include mortice knobs, lever handles, bolts, locks, escutcheons, espagnolettes, push plates, knockers, letterboxes – even coat hooks.

And just as a well-chosen accessory can transform an otherwise dull outfit, so too with hardware. It is well worth taking time and trouble over what may seem like very small matters – look at salvaged as well as new – as an ill-considered choice can compromise the overall feel and function of a space.

02

Electrical fittings

Instead of boring white plastic, why not consider electrical sockets (outlets) that you can paint to match the wall so they disappear? Or light switches with Perspex (Plexiglas) plates, which reveal the surrounding wall finish beneath and minimize the impact of the switch?
I love 'dolly' switches, shaped like a tiny doll. Switches and socket plates come in many different finishes, too, from brushed chrome to antiqued bronze, so exercise your power to choose.

03

04

01
A door and its frame become handy vehicles for saturated colour.

02
A large-format hammered finish is given to this door, a promise of the elemental aesthetic of the bathroom that is beyond.

03
The refined modernity of these light switches is a cool contrast to the 'wild' timber wall panels on which they are mounted.

04
The utilitarian beauty of electrical components is celebrated in these light fixtures that I spotted while filming in a *Masseria* in Puglia, Italy.

01

A fireplace chock-full of candles is a resourceful way of emulating the theatrics of a real fire.

02

The precision of a, now classic, hole-in-the-wall fireplace is balanced by a pair of hand-thrown pots in the same black-as-pitch colour as the fire's recess.

03

A fireplace is wrought from architectural planes, the precision of which accentuates the rough surfaces of the logs.

01

02

Fireplaces

No matter what kind of fireplace you have – an open fire, a vented gas fire, a flueless gas fire, a solid-fuel or wood-burning stove, or even a gel fire – there will be decisions to be made about the way it is 'dressed'. These range from the choice of fire surround to the hearth material and fire basket.

Traditional fireplace materials include stone, plaster, wood, brick, marble, cast iron and tile. Modern times mean that 'modern' materials and finishes – such as engineered stone, coloured or mirrored glass, slate, steel and concrete – can be added to this list.

More coolly simple ideas are to be considered, too. It is not necessary to buy a conventional fire surround. I once modernized a fireplace by simply replacing an old, rather florid and over-large design with three restrained planes of a beautiful marble, the character being in the material rather than how it was tricked up.

Hearths need to withstand heat, however. I learned my lesson when the too-thin sheet of slate I had fitted cracked, dramatically, once my fire heated up.

Designs for fire baskets range from traditional to contemporary and come in different finishes, too, from cast iron to modern stainless steel.

In recent times, hole-in-the-wall fireplaces have become popular, but I fear these will date in much the same way as 1970s lava lamps. Though they fit perfectly in similarly ascetic spaces, they contrast oddly with those that are not. A fireplace is a focal point, a role that an often too small rectangular recess struggles to perform. And more elaborate renditions of the hole-in-the-wall idea, in which stone or metal is used to dress the thing up, contradict the original, pure concept.

Built-in furniture

A sound investment in homes where space is tight, built-in furniture will make the most of the space you have. It also implies some degree of customization. Built-in elements such as wardrobes and bookcases can be semi-bespoke, whereby a 'system' of built-in furniture is adapted to your home; or they can be fully bespoke, whereby you can specify every feature, from finish to mechanism.

I often specify built-in wardrobes in clients' bedrooms, but the potentially oppressive mass must be reduced by making them visually recessive. This can be achieved by facing the doors with reflective materials, or finishing them in the same way as the surrounding walls. If there are mouldings in the room, such as a coving detail or a skirting (baseboard), this usually looks better if it is continued around the face of the wardrobes rather than cut off at the point where they begin. The same caution applies to any similar full-height storage piece. See built-in kitchens (page 197) for notes on quality.

furnishings

Like most elements in the home, furnishings – that is, furniture and soft furnishings – have a role to play in both aesthetics and practicality. Furnishings can greatly contribute to the overall look of a space, and not just in terms of surface finish. For example, in smaller spaces, furniture that is open, lightweight and even transparent will allow a more fluid flow of space and light. Furniture that will be in prolonged contact with the body, such as armchairs and beds, has the potential to support and envelop. These items are the part of the home that can give you a hug – or a pain in the neck – and should be chosen with the idiosyncrasies of personal body shape in mind.

Furniture

From metal to plastic and from wood to glass, furniture can be made of any material that can do the job, but in all cases you should properly evaluate the quality before you make a purchase. Do not be afraid to try out and even turn pieces upside down in showrooms or shops, inspecting joints and construction details, which should be 'clean' and unyielding. Lie on beds and sit on sofas. Lean back in dining chairs, which should remain rigid.

Furniture incorporating cupboards can be judged by the way doors swing, which should be smooth and firm. Drawers should open and close smoothly, and their bases should be rigid. Check the quality of any hardware, which should be firmly fixed. Any exposed glass edges should be bevelled.

When investing in children's furniture – beds, desks, storage items – bear in mind that their preferences are capricious, and they grow up quickly, so themes should be avoided. Pieces that can be adapted as their needs change will be the best value.

The best upholstered sofas and armchairs are constructed out of a high-quality metal or solid hardwood frame. Comfort and support are provided by either springs or foam. The best-quality springs are those that are hand-tied, while more affordable alternatives are called 'sagless' springs, though these are not quite as flexible. The quality of upholstered furniture padded with foam is always indicated by price as well as comfort. The least expensive kind of foam-filled furniture can lose as much as 20 per cent of its firmness in the first three months.

In a good piece of upholstered furniture, you should not be able to feel the frame through the fabric. The joints in the frame

01

A playful interpretation of traditional joinery motifs creates a freestanding cabinet, which sits comfortably next to built-in furniture elements.

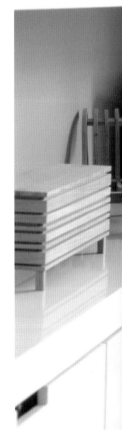

A bench at the end of this bed provides not only a visual full stop but also a useful spot on which to sit when removing shoes.

should be firm, the webbing – woven tapes – beneath should be well fixed and the stitching should be perfect. Any buttons should be stitched all the way through to the back instead of just to the fabric. The feet should be firmly attached. If there is a pattern on the upholstery fabric it should match at the seams.

Where new wood is used in a piece of furniture, check that it is from an FSC-approved source. Where wood composites are used, such as plywood or MDF (medium-density fibreboard), be sure to check that these use adhesives and resins that contain low to no VOCs. Pieces largely made from wood composites will not last as long as those made from solid wood.

The lifespan of a piece of furniture not only has environmental implications but also has implications for your pocket and even for safety, so spend as much as you can afford. Sometimes second-hand, vintage (which is posh second-hand) or antique furniture will be equally, if not more, affordable and much better-made – not to mention well tested.

Be careful not to buy furniture that is too big for a room – a scale plan will help you avoid this common mistake – or too big to fit through your doors or up the stairs. Some new furniture can take 12 weeks or more to be delivered, and longer if you place your order with a manufacturer based in Europe close to the August shutdown.

Beds
Bed manufacturers recommend you buy as big a bed as the bedroom can comfortably contain. However, the best way to judge how

large a size you need is to add about 20cm (8in) to the length of the tallest 'bed user'. Width is a matter of how cosy you like to be.

To work out how supportive a bed will be, lie down on it and slip your hand between the small of your back and the mattress. If the fit is very snug, the mattress may be too soft.

Most mattresses need to be turned regularly in order to maintain shape. There are 'no-turn' mattresses available but most of these will last only half as long as the equivalent standard mattress – in most cases 'no-turn' is just a marketing gimmick.

The best mattresses on the market are either made of high-quality natural latex or are well sprung – the more springs there are and the thicker they are, the better the support. Hand-tied pocket springs take first prize, while open springs are more affordable, though less flexible. The most

hypoallergenic mattresses are those made out of natural materials.

Memory-foam mattresses have become popular and are considered to be uniquely supportive, but the first products on the market were made of polyurethane, which will leach very detectable VOCs. As a result, manufacturers have developed 'eco' memory foam. This significantly reduces the amount of petrochemicals, by either substituting plant-based alternatives or having a large recycled content.

Divan beds, composed of an upholstered box spring and matching mattress, are the most space-efficient. If replacing a mattress or a bed frame, be sure that they will match up by asking the respective suppliers. The slats on a good-quality bed frame should be no more than 4cm (1½in) apart.

02
A pair of 1950's chairs are
upholstered in a classic chintz,
where two well-recognized styles
combine to create something
entirely new.

Soft furnishings

Fabrics will often make the sole
contribution to pattern in a room, and it
can be temptingly easy to stick to just one.
But patterns can be successfully mixed to
create lively, confident comfort. For a
harmonious ensemble ensure that whatever
patterns you choose clearly contrast in
terms of style of repeat, scale or texture but
share a colour element.

I think of furnishings as the 'team leader'
of a room. A well-chosen fabric can tie
together what may seem discordant
features, by echoing the colours, textures
and patterns in a single, unifying element.
However, you must exercise subtlety, to
avoid that 'show home' look.

Altering some of your soft furnishings,
whether it is the upholstery on a well-loved
sofa, the slipcovers on your dining chairs or
simply some pillow covers, is one of the
least expensive ways to refresh a home –
the textile equivalent of a pot of paint.
There is a world of fabrics to choose from,
but avoid those that are loosely woven as
they will snag.

Instead of new fabrics you may want to
try vintage, or simply second-hand. Not
only might they be cost-effective options,
not to mention environmentally friendly,
but vintage fabrics can add noticeable
personality to a room scheme. The same
applies to what is called 'passementerie',
a charming word for trimmings. An
alternative to passementerie is to add
piping around the edge of upholstery,
in matching or contrasting fabric, which
will give the piece crisp form.

Most fabrics are sensitive to sunlight,
and silk will comprehensively deteriorate
in time. Some fabrics are more resistant
than others and some will have been
chemically treated to be so. Certain kinds
of cotton are naturally resistant. UV
damage can also be ameliorated by the
kind of glass you have in your home.
If the occupants of your home include
children, pets, or someone who is just a
bit clumsy (you included) – or if you are
tempted to select very pale fabrics – then
washable materials and loose slipcovers
for seating will be helpful.

Soft furnishings can sometimes be
subject to a great deal of chemical
treatment, specifically with fire- and
stain-retardants. Brominated fire-
retardants are known to be hormone
disruptors. Any toxic effect of stain-
retardants is yet to be decisively proved
but they are known 'bioaccumulators'
– that is, they take longer to be excreted
by an organism (such as us) than they
take to be ingested.

Not all upholstered furniture or
furnishing fabrics will be treated, of
course, so it is worth asking your
supplier about it. A natural fabric, such
as wool, has inherent fire- and stain-
resistance. So does leather, but there are
environmental factors to consider here
(see page 183).

Hemp, whether raw or coloured with
natural dyes, is considered the most
environmentally friendly fabric, as it
can be grown locally and absorbs carbon
while doing so. Hemp shower curtains, in
particular, are a good option, as they are
a VOC-free – and 'non-cling' – alternative
to plastic.

01

Bath-time privacy is satisfied by
a Hollywood classic in this clever
design for a blind.

02

Vertical blinds are only ever
acceptable in offices or Modernist
homes. This bedroom, falling into
the latter category, means the
vertical blinds work very well here,
providing privacy from the outside
and views from the inside.

Window treatments

Your choice of window treatment will depend partly on how satisfied you are with the level of daylight, privacy and insulation a window gives you. The other major factor is the decorative contribution different types of window dressing and materials can make to a room.

If you need to make the most of daylight, translucent dressings will obviously be the best choice. A window can be made to appear bigger by fitting a much larger translucent dressing across it. Where both light and privacy need to be maximized, Venetian blinds are a good solution.

Shades and blinds are less bulky than curtains, which makes them useful in tight spaces, though vertical blinds should only be used in very sharp, modern homes or

offices. The best-known are roller, reverse roller and Roman shades and Venetian and pinoleum blinds (made of very thin strands of timber). Roman shades and pinoleum blinds are particularly well suited to odd-shaped windows. Shoji shades (rice paper stretched over a wooden frame) and curtains on portière rods (hinged to the side so the curtains open like doors) suit glass doors.

Where a window has a radiator beneath it, a blind or shade is really the only option. A curtain would only insulate you from the source of heat. At any rate, curtains always look better full-length, even on short windows.

Some blinds insulate against heat loss. Honeycomb blinds, where the fabric is pleated to create a series of insulating cells, is one such example.

For warmth, however, it is hard to beat curtains, which can be lined or even double-lined (also known as interlining). Lining in a contrasting fabric, which should be UV-resistant, will, like a contrasting lining in a smart suit, add an element of surprise and contribute to the impression of your home from the outside. Lining improves the hang of a curtain fabric, and blackout lining, which comes in colours other than black, will give maximum protection from dawn's light.

Curtains can be hung on either a pole or a track (rod). Poles and finials add another dimension to creative expression, as do the 'acorns' on roman shades, which can be replaced by anything you can grab hold of, within reason. Tracks make no decorative contribution, other than allowing for pleats, the top of which can be concealed behind a pelmet (cornice) or valance. A quietly dramatic lighting effect is to conceal a low-temperature light source behind the pelmet.

Both curtains and shades come ready-made, while customization, though more expensive, allows greater choice. If you have fallen for a very expensive fabric that is not quite within your budget, consider using it as a contrasting trim on a fabric that is.

When measuring for curtains or shades, allow for mechanisms, hems, any tabs and the amount by which the pole or track extends beyond the sides of the window. To guarantee generous pleats, curtains should be about twice as wide as the length of the pole or track, though the exact amount of fullness you need depends on the heading (top treatment).

To improve fall, all fabrics can be stiffened – helpful when having bed valances made up.

02

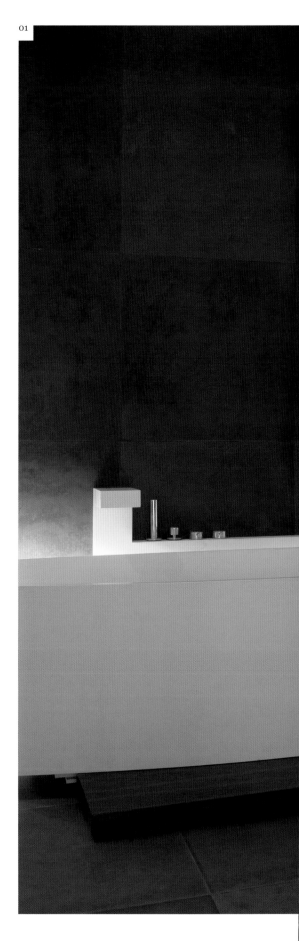

Lighting

The most pleasurable lighting schemes are those that illuminate while preserving a degree of shadow. Shadow suggests depth and privacy, while light means you can see what you are doing and guards against fatigue and even depression.

Natural daylight can be manipulated and amplified using reflective surfaces – a mirrored window recess will draw daylight into a room. Or it can be diffused through translucent materials to spread daylight's reach.

Artificial light offers a greater variety of effects. Ambient light is general background light – what the 20th-century lighting designer Richard Kelly described as 'a snowy morning in open country' – where light is infinite and consistent. Task lighting, Kelly said, 'tells people what to look at', like 'your airplane seat light', while decorative light celebrates 'the sparkle'.

Winter usually means that artificial light must compensate for the lack of natural light, during the day as well as at night. The least depressing way to do this is to install a number of different concealed ambient light sources, as this creates the kind of sharp contrasts reminiscent of a sunny day. This is one of the reasons we love those days so much.

One method is to recess floor lights behind a voile curtain, which will diffuse the light in the same way as natural light would. Lights can also be concealed beneath furniture or behind pelmets. A light source fitted to the top of a wardrobe, or behind a sheet of translucent material, will 'dematerialize' what is above or behind, making it seem like there is more space than there actually is. Vertical uplighting will always visually heighten any space, while lighting on the horizontal plane, such as side lighting, will make a space appear wider.

Light fixtures

Once you have worked out what kind of lighting you want, you will then need to decide what kind of light fixtures will do the job. Lighting, because of the enormous range on offer and effects achievable, can be rather complicated, and if you are after something sophisticated a specialist lighting designer will be able to advise. Alternatively, a mix of relatively simple ambient and task lights will give you a greater degree of flexibility, and effects can be further enhanced by fitting dimmer switches.

For lighting that is fixed to walls, ceilings or even floors, the first thing to decide is whether you would prefer a luminaire rather than a bulb and shade arrangement. A luminaire is an all-in-one light fixture, complete with bulb (technically, and confusingly, called a lamp), a reflector for directing the light, an aperture (with or without a lens) and the outer shell, or housing, both to protect and to align the lamp. Recessed spotlights are luminaires, as are side lights and floor lights. There are many kinds of luminaires that perform in different ways, so the best thing is to visit a good lighting showroom where all the options are displayed.

01
Concealed, ambient light enhances
the amniotic atmosphere in this
contemporary bathroom.

If you decide to opt for any pendant lights or table lamps, wall lights or floor lamps, the kind of shade you choose can add to the effect. Shades lined in gold will softly gild white light, and those with perforations or patterns that are only noticeable when a light is turned on add charming surprise.

In wet areas like bathrooms the type of fixture you choose will probably be restricted by regulations, as water and electricity are a lethal mix. Fixtures with IP (ingress protection) ratings are what you need to look out for in Europe and Asia; in North America the same system is determined by NEMA (National Electrical Manufacturers Association).

Pendant lights should be hung 700–800mm (27–31in) above a dining or kitchen table. If you want to suspend a pendant light any higher, consider one with a diffuser to conceal the bulb, or use a crown-silvered bulb that will direct light upward, reducing glare. But the closer a light fixture is to the table, the greater the sense of intimacy (providing it does not block sight lines).

The best height for table lamps is when the lower edge of the lamp shade is in line with the eye level of the seated person. This will allow the light to illuminate whatever they are reading, without creating glare. A painting can be illuminated with a classic picture light or, more minimally, with a spotlight. The centre of the spotlight beam should ideally hit the centre of the painting at an angle of 30–45 degrees to the vertical.

Types of bulb

Bulbs present another level of choices. Tungsten and halogen are incandescent, meaning that the lamp consists of a hot wire – the filament – contained in a glass bulb. Tungsten is not used so much these days as it is energy-inefficient, but it gives a lovely yellow glow. Halogen provides a brighter, whiter, more sparkly light and is a little more energy-efficient, though a bulb is ruined if it is touched. Low-voltage bulbs, another kind of incandescent bulb, deliver a more targeted beam of light. They are usually an integral component of a luminaire.

Energy-saving bulbs are the future and are available as compact fluorescent lights (CFLs) or light-emitting diodes (LEDs). Good-quality fittings (the only ones worth using) tend to be more expensive in terms of upfront cost, but are actually less expensive in the long run as they last much longer and use less energy.

Because LEDs are tiny, they are often used decoratively – to transform a ceiling into a 'starry sky', for example, or in 'decolume' strips. Resembling a string of Christmas-tree lights but more robust, these make an effective concealed edge-to-edge source of strip lighting. They come in different colours, too. They are also used in more commonly recognized luminaires, such as recessed spots.

The drawback with energy-saving bulbs – and fluorescent strip lights can be included in this category – is that the quality of light can be quite cold. However, improvements are constantly being made. An improvement on fluorescent strips, which are inexpensive both to buy and to run, is to slip over candy-coloured gels. Yum.

01

01
Strips of pink neon indicate the bar is open.

02
Pendant light fittings, like a fleet of benign space craft, hover in formation in a double-height dining space.

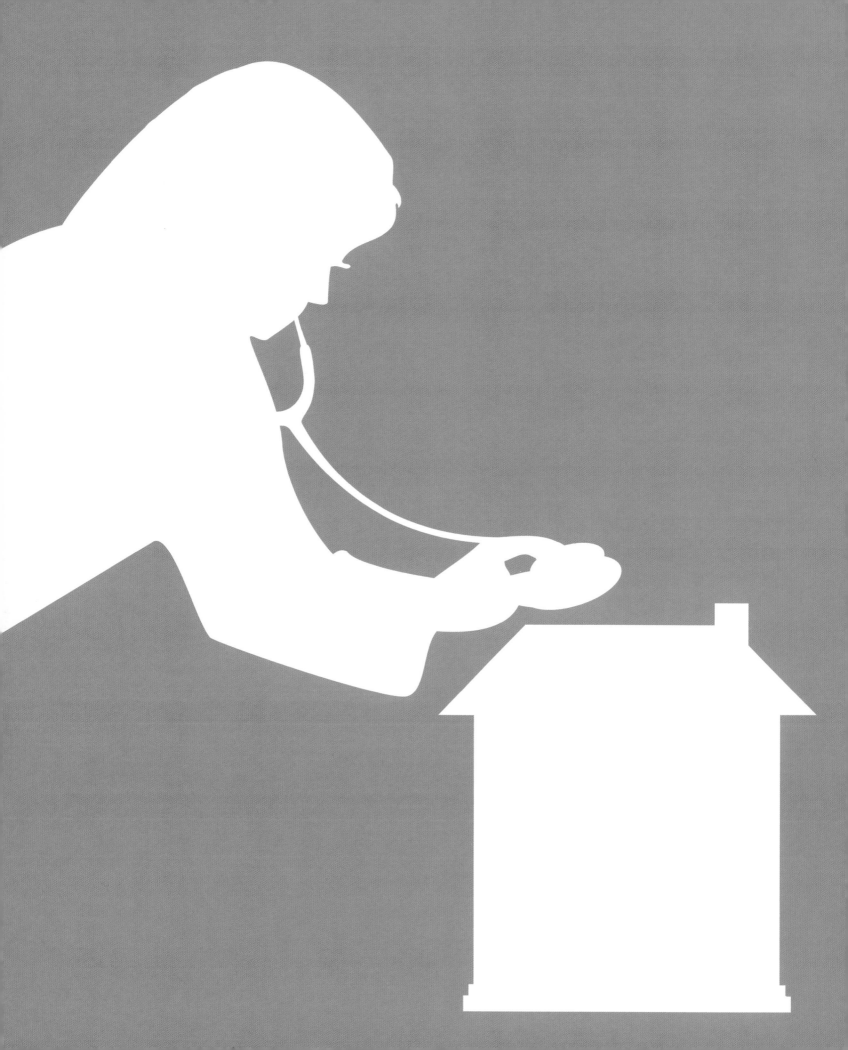

6
troubleshooting

6

troubleshooting

While many of the problems you might have with a space will be specific to you, your household and the architecture of your home, there are some commonly experienced challenges to which there are a variety of solutions.

TOO SMALL

01

Mirrors may be an obvious solution to a small or dark space, but they are a fail-safe way to make it seem larger and brighter. Keeping them nicely polished is another matter.

When designing a home, insufficient space is the most common frustration, in terms of both practical use and visual impression. Practical solutions to this can be divided into those that physically add space and those that cleverly find extra space in unexpected places.

The first type, adding space, is self-explanatory, but before you make that investment do make sure you thoroughly assess the space you already have against what you really need (see Chapter 4). You may, for example, discover you don't need to add on to your home after all. And if you do decide to add space, think carefully about how it will connect with your existing space – it is surprising how uncommon common sense like this is.

Hidden space

To discover those spaces that are currently hiding from you, the 'knock knock' method must be deployed. Just knock on all the surfaces in your home – walls, floors, ceilings, staircases – to see if they might be hollow. If any are, this is your extra space. Your ceiling might be suspended, so you could remove it to create more height.

Quite often pipes, such as a downpipe in the corner of a room, will be boxed in more generously than is strictly required, so remove a small section in an unobtrusive area to check. If you have a suspended floor you might be able to store things beneath, nautical-style, with doors in the floor. The risers in a staircase can be converted into bookshelves. To find more space inside 'the box' it is necessary to think outside of it.

Dressing up

To create the impression of more space requires a bit of theatre. Here are some tricks from the interior designer's dressing-up chest that you can try:

- Lay strip flooring or tile on the diagonal, instead of front to back or side to side, to abstract the vanishing point when you view a space.
- Use lots of mirrors. I know: sounds obvious. But use them with panache and a cunning eye, mirroring an entire wall, the full face of a door, the reveals in a window casement or the rear of recesses. Even a small amount of mirror can create a huge effect.

01

This kitchen/diner uses a box of clever tricks to amplify the impression of space; the pull-out larder units make the most accessible use of storage space; the use of diagonal lines in the storage wall play with perspective, as does the image of a city skyline that forms the splashback.

02

A staircase becomes a handy chest of drawers.

03

The lower half of the staircase here consists of elements that have multifunctional uses: table and sofa to name just two.

Don't forget that mirror comes in different colours, and it can even be etched and treated. The same effects can be created with coloured glass.

☐ If a ceiling feels too low, use vertical motifs to visually raise it, such as a wallpaper with a vertical pattern, vertically shaped wall lights or an arrangement of long, thin decorative accessories wall-mounted vertically.

☐ In the same way that vertical motifs give the impression of height, horizontal motifs will give the impression of more width.

☐ If you can spare lateral space, another way to 'raise' a low ceiling is to recess lighting at the top of the walls. Build a false wall, which should stop just short of the ceiling. In the space at the top between the real wall and the false wall you can conceal lighting – I would recommend a strip of light, such as a decolume strip, or even a thin fluorescent tube in a tinted gel sleeve, to warm the quality of usually cold fluorescent light. When switched on, the light will dissolve the corner between wall and ceiling.

☐ The previous method can be applied to corners of a room, where a strategically placed recessed floor light will dissolve the boundaries of a corner.

☐ Furnish a compact room with pieces that are at least to scale and, ideally, neatly slimline. This way, the limited space that you have will still feel airy and comfortable.

☐ Likewise, furniture on legs – for example, a bedstead instead of a divan – and pieces made of transparent or perforated materials will allow light to penetrate, and permit views across and through a space, so that the full measure of it can be appreciated.

☐ Mirroring the rear planes of any recesses, such as the alcoves flanking a fireplace, is not the only way to create the impression of more space. An alternative is to paint them in a shade that is slightly darker than the shade on adjacent walls. In so doing you will be creating false shadow, and therefore a feeling of depth.

☐ One of my favourite ways of giving the impression of more space is to incorporate large paintings or photographs of landscapes. Abstract works that express similar spatial qualities will also be effective.

☐ The most radical way to make a small space feel bigger is to remove some walls, but be careful not to go mad. Some walls will be holding your building up, so if you take these down you may end up removing more than you planned. If you are unsure which are your load-bearing walls and which are not, knock on each of them. A hollow report usually indicates a partition wall, which is one you can tear down. To be doubly sure consult a structural engineer, who will also be able to advise on the rather more complicated, and costly, measures that can be taken to remove load-bearing walls.

If you do remove walls, the functions of different parts of the resulting space can be reinforced not only through the kind of furniture and fittings installed, but also through the use of different colours and types of floor finishes, and through changes in level. If you feel nervous about removing an entire wall, try cutting it in half. A short wall will delineate a space while also opening it up and making it open plan, at least from waist level upward.

01
Shelving is punctuated by coloured light boxes that turn up the volume of light in this room.

02
A lower-ground-floor living room is illuminated by natural daylight drawn down through a light well at the perimeter of the ground floor above.

03
Any attempt to brighten this dark, Georgian hallway with light colours and bright lights would have meant losing out on its ready-made, romantic atmosphere, so I made it darker still by using a London-gloom deep grey/green navigated by a scarlet stair carpet.

TOO DARK

Before you begin to contemplate 'solutions' for a space that you feel is too dark, it is worth taking a moment to consider the delights of inhabiting a dark and cosy space, a space of deep colour and fathomless texture. Certain spaces even invite darkness: a bedroom, for example. But if, after you have thought this one through, you still feel you need to make your space brighter, here are some ways to exaggerate natural light and to cleverly employ artificial light to emulate daylight, too:

- ☐ Increase the size of your windows. Just check with your local planners first, to make sure you do not require any planning permission. You may also need to liaise with a professional structural engineer.
- ☐ Replace solid doors with glazed doors, so that your dark space is illuminated by borrowed light from adjacent rooms, or from outside.
- ☐ Fit the window recess with mirror, which will reflect the natural light coming through. For the same reason, they are often painted white.
- ☐ Fitting a window with a much larger translucent shade or blind, perhaps even as large as the full height and width of the wall in which the window sits, will diffuse the natural daylight penetrating that window across the breadth of the curtain. This device can be given a fillip with the addition of small spotlights recessed into the floor beneath a full-length translucent curtain. On dark, wintry or overcast days you will be seduced into thinking there is more daylight flooding through your windows into the room than there really is.

- ☐ Concealed artificial light sources will always make for a more sophisticated way of illuminating a dark space than more obvious floor and table lamps or ceiling- and wall-mounted fixtures, though a combination of both is the most desirable.
- ☐ Glossy materials always amplify light, whether they are dark or light.

01
Glossy surfaces, white paint,
see-through furniture and a light
well all play their part in the
experience of light and space.

02
A fully glazed partition wall allows
light to penetrate floors above and
below, as well as visually extending
the perimeter of this space.

02

TOO NOISY

Noise is the difference between those sounds that are welcome and those that are not. It can even affect our health. Typical city noise, at approximately 70dB (decibels), can cause mental and physical fatigue. And so-called 'background' noise, such as the sound of an air-conditioning unit, can interfere with sleep, digestion and thought, too. (It is therefore ironic that many modern restaurants are uncomfortably noisy, owing to design decisions that failed to consider how a space would feel in operation as much as how it looked on the drawing board.)

A soundless environment, however, is a dead one. Sensory deprivation experiments have shown that if the senses are denied stimulus, anxiety shortly follows.

The modern home can hum with noise. It may originate internally from appliances and audio equipment, and externally from vehicle traffic, lawnmowers and aircraft, not to mention noisy neighbours and barking dogs.

In order to minimize noise it is important to understand not just its source but also its behaviour. Sound can travel through air and via structure, and can reverberate and be amplified by the kinds of finishes we choose for our homes.

Where sound travels through air, sound insulation can be approached in much the same way as heat insulation, the solutions having the same effect. First check your windows – ill-fitting windows are the most common cause of noise in the home.

02

01

If they are loose you should appoint a specialist company to refurbish them to create a tight seal. You could also consider replacing the glass with specialist noise-reducing glass such as Pilkington Optiphon. A radical alternative is to replace the entire window, but this should be your last resort.

An additional solution to unwanted sound is to install specially designed 'acoustic curtains' across windows. To save on cost, these can be sourced second-hand from commercial properties, such as hotels, and then used to line new, full-length curtains in a design that harmonizes with the rest of your home. To optimize the effect, acoustic curtains should be fitted across the entire wall in which a window sits, edge to edge.

A less technical and, potentially, less expensive version of acoustic curtains is a pair of ordinary curtains that are double-lined, made of a dense fabric, such as velvet or weighty canvas.

The other major culprit, when it comes to noisy space, is hard, flat, smooth surfaces. If your preference is for hard, flat, smooth floors and walls, just ensure there is plenty of insulation beneath. You can then break up floor surfaces with rugs, and wall surfaces with artwork, which will reduce the amount of echo.

Other sound-dampening solutions could include:

☐ Installing houseplants.
☐ Papering or upholstering walls.
☐ Fitting a suspended ceiling.

☐ Adding soft furnishings, such as upholstered furniture or cushions, or even a tablecloth in an echoing dining room (a good rule of thumb is that at least 25 per cent of a room should be covered in textiles).
☐ Mounting noisy appliances on sheets of thick rubber matting.

For areas where sound is pivotal to the function and enjoyment of a space, for example a media room where you listen to music or watch films and television, you might want to consider employing professional sound specialists. They can fit soundproofing panels to walls and ceilings and even soundproofing devices around recessed spotlights, all of which can be concealed and decorated into your home.

TOO BIG

01

An almost triple-height space is given some sense of intimacy, while preserving impressive volume, through the use of a remarkable chandelier and a softening and connecting voile window dressing.

02

An inventive wall-painting scheme visually lowers the tall ceiling in this large bedroom.

Acquiring a home that is 'too big' is a nice problem to have, but just because it is nice, it doesn't mean it is any less of a challenge. 'Too big' is a problem I come across frequently when I work on spaces like loft apartments – open-plan, single-level homes of 200 square metres (2,000 sq ft) or more – where lavish volume is desirable but so is livability. The solution lies chiefly in the way that you furnish. Here are some guidelines:

☐ Furniture needs to be in scale – this is where you can indulge in large, generously proportioned pieces and sculpture, or even eccentric items of architectural salvage.

☐ An alternative is to group standard-sized pieces of furniture, to create areas of intimacy within the expanse.

☐ Dark colours and big textures will also create cosiness, while preserving the full scope of the dimensions.

☐ Using a dark colour on a ceiling and taking it down along the top of the walls to nominal picture-rail height will give the impression that a very high ceiling is lower than it actually is. Nevertheless, high ceilings do not lend themselves to intimacy, in which case groups of low-level furniture illuminated by low-level lighting – suspended pendants or table lamps – will be the trick to use here.

01

A long, thin space is shaped into more manageable proportions using two visual tricks, one of which has two interpretations. First, a sideboard is installed at one of the short ends of the room to visually draw that elevation toward the centre point. Second, the concept of fragmentation to create cohesion is expressed in the collection of pictures centralized along one of the long walls and also in the collection of variously suspended and, crucially, vertically shaped pendant light fittings, all perfectly positioned at the centre of the space. The use of a single pendant or painting would simply not have the same cohesive effect.

02

A line of gargantuan lamp shades glorify the volume of space available in this dining area while introducing an essential dining companion: intimacy.

7

mechanics

7
mechanics

In 1923 the architect Le Corbusier famously claimed that the home is 'a machine for living in', heralding a new age of architecture. Industrial methods began to be favoured over decorative craft in the pursuit of new, healthier democratic dwellings and, ultimately, a utopian society – where crime was banished and everyone had a light tan.

Le Corbusier's ambitious theories may be nearly antique, and not to everyone's taste aesthetically, but the fact remains that he was on to something. Contemporary homes may not comprehensively adopt the pure 'anti-aesthetics' of machines, but they have become increasingly mechanized as technology has developed and become widely accessible. And not only does modern technology facilitate basic functions, or even make our homes more entertaining, but it is the key to making them more 'resource-efficient', saving on costs 'in service' as well as being ecologically sensitive.

The breadth of operations available to us, combined with the fact that necessary wires and pipes are always best concealed, means it is vital to think through your needs carefully prior to installing any final finishes or fixtures. Otherwise, you could find living with the consequences pure frustration.

Simply re-covering walls and floors can present an ideal opportunity to make other improvements. For example, a new living-room floor offers the potential for adding floor sockets (outlets), liberating seating and lamps from a room's perimeter.

PLUMBING

If you are investing in a new bathroom complete with new taps (faucets), you will be wasting your money if you have not first confirmed whether your plumbing will provide sufficient hot water and, in some countries, whether your water pressure is compatible. A plumber or heating engineer will be able to tell you whether your system, from hot water to heating, is up to scratch throughout your home, as well as advising on regulations.

If it is not, there are a number of options, from solar-heated water to a pressurized system. The viability of each will depend on how many outlets you have that draw from the water supply (such as the number of taps, shower heads, washing machines, and suchlike), your local water system, the type of property you live in and your budget.

In hard-water areas it is well worth installing a water softener. These are not inexpensive but will save you money in the long run by protecting your pipes, and indeed all surfaces that come into contact with water, from the build-up of limescale.

If you are embarking on a significant refurbishment, you could install a water-recovery mechanism, such as a 'grey water harvester' where, for example, waste water from the washing machine can be used to flush a toilet. More simply, water can be collected from the bath in a water butt located at the base of a downpipe (downspout) and used to water the garden.

ELECTRICITY, TELECOMMUNICATIONS AND DATA

When architects and designers design spaces, one of the documents they produce is an electrical plan. This is a scale plan indicating the site, specification and quantity of all proposed light fixtures, sockets (outlets), light switches, telecom and television points, and security systems such as video entry systems, alarms and panic buttons. You can do this, too. Sketching out your own plan will help you to focus on your requirements. For example, telecommunications and data points for telephones, personal computers and entertainment systems can be located anywhere you want them, even in the bathroom, but you will probably need time to think about all the possibilities.

Light switches can be located at any height that is convenient or simply looks right to you, a fact frequently overlooked. In a room illuminated solely by table or floor lamps, it will be easier to turn them on with a switch at the door as you enter. You may also find a switch located at your bedside useful, to turn off all the lights in your bedroom without having to emerge from the cosiness of bed.

Dimmer switches can adjust light levels to create a particular mood, and automated light switches can be pre-programmed to specific settings to create certain atmospheres. However, systems like these are only worth the investment if you have a big home or an unusually large collection of light fixtures.

APPLIANCES

Life would be very hard work without appliances, an amorphous term for those machines that facilitate domestic life and minimize domestic chores – ovens and washing machines, wine cabinets and chiller drawers, even trash compactors.

While there is a movement afoot to promote the idea of 'smart' appliances that can email you when they have finished their work, or tell you when you have run out of milk, the best kind of appliances are those that perform core functions effectively and efficiently. They provide what you really need without the cost of those functions you do not. In some countries, appliances are rated according to their energy-efficiency rating, with a top rating being, for example, AA+.

Many appliances can be bought for competitive prices on the internet, but do inspect them in the flesh before making a commitment. Remember that if you are planning to integrate your appliances into cabinets, such as in a built-in kitchen, you will need to buy specially adapted appliances.

Once you have made your decision, the appliances will need to be connected to electricity, gas, water or oil. This must be factored into your overall plans so that pipes and wiring can be chased and ducted as unobtrusively as possible. Some powerful appliances will require a specific kind of safety switching.

Centralized vacuum systems will make dragging the vacuum cleaner around the house the stuff of memories, so are worth considering. However, they will require a considerable amount of duct work.

CLIMATE CONTROL

One of the many benefits of a home is the ability to control your environment, and that includes the air, through what is known as climate control or HVAC – heating, ventilation and air conditioning. The efficacy of any heating and cooling system will be as good as the insulation in your home, as well as the ventilation. Therefore, if you are upgrading your systems it is also wise to check how well sealed your windows are, the level of insulation in your perimeter walls and roof, and the home's ventilation. Insulation and ventilation may appear contradictory features, but air temperature will be better controlled if perimeters are insulated, while controlled ventilation will allow air to circulate and any mould- or mildew-causing moisture to escape.

HEATING

A home can be heated in a variety of different ways. Often the best solution is a combination of methods.

Radiators

Radiators are heated by hot water (called a 'wet' system) or electricity. It is even possible to source electrically powered 'wet' radiators. In the end, the system you choose will be decided by installation and running costs. Electricity is less disruptive and therefore less costly to install, but more expensive than a wet system to run.

Factors to take into account when choosing radiators are performance and good looks. However, 'feature' radiators, in the shape of a sprung coil or a triffid-like house plant, for example, are best avoided. Radiators should complement your decor, not jump out screaming for attention.

Radiators heated by hot water require valves, but there is no need to have your carefully chosen radiator compromised by a purely utilitarian fitting. Valves are available in elegant designs that can offer both manual and thermostatic control and a choice of straight, angled or double-angled, according to how you wish to mount your radiator. The thermostatic control of each radiator means that you can fine-tune the warmth of each room, improving overall energy efficiency.

Classic cast-iron column radiators look good in just about any environment – contemporary or traditional – though they can be quite bulky and heavy. Aluminium radiators are much lighter and can be wall-mounted. Radiators in tubular steel allow for long, tall or low shapes. Flat-panel radiators can be the least intrusive, especially when recessed into a wall, but if heated by hot water they are only compatible with certain hot-water systems.

Towel radiators (towel warmers) can be installed as part of a central heating system. They can be electrically powered only or can be 'dual fuel', whereby they come on with your central heating in the winter but can be powered by electricity in the summer. A towel radiator will rarely be sufficient to heat a bathroom, so an additional radiator, or electric underfloor heating, will need to be installed. The latter is more space- and energy-efficient.

Some radiators can be precoated with a colour or metallic finish of your choice or painted on site. Long, low radiators can be recessed into the floor, with a grille fitted above – called trench radiators, these are often installed at draughty thresholds.

The number and size of radiators you will need for a space is best calculated by your plumber or heating engineer, who will also be able to advise you on optimum location. It is said that you should place a radiator beneath a window, as this will be the coldest spot, but if you have very well-insulated windows and walls you do not need to follow this rule – you can put radiators anywhere you like, which will give you greater flexibility.

If siting a radiator beneath a window is the only option open to you, and you really want full-length curtains too, your radiator needs to be 30 per cent larger than it would otherwise be.

Underfloor heating

The two great benefits of underfloor heating are that its source is concealed, maximizing usable floor space and minimizing interruption to your decor, and it is more efficient to run. The consistent distribution of heat means that the system can be run at lower temperatures than radiators, making them an ideal fit with low-heat-producing ground- or air-source heat pumps, resulting in lower bills. However, the performance of underfloor heating depends on how well the floor is insulated, because heat can be lost through the base instead of being channelled into your home.

Underfloor heating systems can be used with most kinds of flooring. All stone and clay-based tiles are particularly suited to this method of heating. Linoleum and vinyl should not be thicker than 5mm (¼in). Carpets should not be thicker than 12mm (½in), with an underlay of no more than 3mm (⅛in). A glued carpet will allow for an increased heat output, but do ensure that the glue is suitable for this application. In the case of wood flooring, seek advice from the manufacturer.

Underfloor heating can be 'zoned', with different areas controllable with thermostatic valves. As with radiators, this improves efficiency and reduces running costs.

Underwall heating

Although underwall heating works on the same principles as underfloor heating, it is less widely used. It is a useful application when floor space needs to be maximized and when it is too disruptive to remove a floor, but as a downside it does not give the kind of even heat distribution that underfloor heating does.

Wet vs dry underfloor-heating systems

Though wet systems are more expensive to install than dry systems, they can be cheaper to run overall, requiring little or no maintenance. They can also be installed alongside most kinds of heat-generating system, from a standard boiler to a biomass boiler and solar panels. Low-temperature-producing systems, such as ground- and air-source heat pumps, are ideal, but do check with respective manufacturers prior to making any investment.

The disadvantages of a wet system is that, unlike a dry system, it requires significant floor 'build-up', consisting of various layers of screeds and insulation. And, of course, any leaks can spell disaster. (This is why it is wise to fit the pipes approximately 100mm (4in) from the outside perimeter of a room, and perhaps even keep a 'map' of their location to avoid nails being banged through in the future.)

The benefit of a dry system is that it takes less time to heat up and costs less to install than a wet system. Electric systems and warm-air systems are the main types, and up-to-date filtration technology has improved air quality by removing the dust and cooking odours that used to compromise the performance of a warm-air system.

However, warm-air systems are difficult to 'retrofit' – that is, install into a property that has already been built. It would necessitate installing suspended ceilings and boxes to conceal ducting.

Open fires and stoves

Human beings have always loved a real fire, from Neanderthal cavemen to modern city-dwellers. And real flame is the only acceptable form. Open fires that burn coal or logs are universally satisfying – full of smoky aromatics, crackle and cinder-glow. They can also be messy and bothersome – and very expensive and disruptive to install if there is no existing chimney.

Gas-fire technology, on the other hand, has developed to provide real and clean flames that can be switched on with a remote control. Heat is an added benefit, though gas fires are not designed to be solitary heat sources.

Flueless gas fires do not even require a chimney, which makes them the most adaptable solution. They are very energy-efficient, too, in that all the warmth generated is directed inside. However, the room in which they are located needs to be fitted with an air brick and have an opening window. Fires like these are fitted with oxygen-depletion sensors that automatically shut off the gas flow if oxygen levels plummet.

Gel fires also provide real flame without the need for a chimney or flue. However, their purpose is solely visual, and in this respect candles are a less toxic and more straightforward option.

Another form of real fire is a stove that burns solid fuel like an open fire but produces more heat. It is still quite messy, however, and needs to be vented outside.

Fires of any kind must be fitted by trained and registered professionals. Fire is dangerous and it needs to be treated with respect.

Cooling

A home can be cooled either passively, using little or no energy, or actively, using systems that require electricity.

Passive systems include the wind towers of ancient Persian design (where hot air naturally escapes from specially designed vents at the top of a building, and cooler air is in turn sucked in at the bottom) and heat pumps. If you have a heat pump warming underfloor heating, it can be reversed to cool in the summer, which makes this the least intrusive method. There is, however, a risk that warm air will condense on a cooler floor, making it dangerously slippery.

Active cooling systems range from conventional air-conditioning systems to evaporative coolers, with a few variations in between. Your choice will be determined by your local climate, budget and the kind of property you live in. Air conditioning cools the same recirculating air using refrigerants. In low-humidity climates, one of a number of cost-effective alternatives to air conditioning would be an evaporative cooling system. This could also be described as the healthy option, because evaporative systems cool fresh air from outside, without the use of hazardous refrigerants, and pump it inside.

Whichever you choose, any cooling 'machine', or evidence thereof, should ideally be concealed, as they are always astonishingly ugly and intrusive. Unfortunately, the internal architecture of your home or your budget may make this impossible, in which case distracting and obscuring tactics must be employed. In any case, a qualified HVAC engineer will be able to advise on all options open to you, as well as the trade-off between implementation and running costs.

Ventilation and air quality

Many heating and cooling systems will be fitted with ventilation and air-quality control systems, which variously circulate air, scrub it of contaminants and control moisture content. Alternatively, air-quality control can be effected using systems independent of cooling and heating, a common example being bathroom extractor fans or vents. Even ceiling and table fans will help to circulate air. Whichever system you feel is best, the rule of concealment – or at least minimizing the visual effect – generally applies and must be borne in mind when making your final decision.

Air quality can also be improved passively by the use of house plants that can filter out contaminants, including VOCs, bioeffluents and airborne microbes. Thus, plants will not only be pretty, but cost-effective and 'green' in every sense. In an average-size home just 10 to 15 plants, grown in 15cm (6in) containers, can do a good job. The most effective are:

□ Boston fern (*Nephrolepis exaltata* 'Bostoniensis')
□ Rubber plant (*Ficus robusta*)
□ Kimberley Queen (*Nephrolepis obliterata*)
□ Areca palm (*Chrysalidocarpus lutescens*)

HOME ENTERTAINMENT

Watching the television or listening to music used to be a simple business. You bought a television or a record player, plugged it in, and enjoyed. These days technology has improved the pleasures of 'home entertainment' exponentially, but the complexity in choice can be bewildering. The best way to make sense of it all is to first think not of what technology you want, but what it is that you really want to do, and where.

If you want to enjoy music, radio, TV, internet and/or video in more than one room, then a multi-room system may be for you. (You can even listen to music or watch TV in the bathroom using special humidity-resistant equipment.) There are a number of ways to achieve this, either with wires or wirelessly. The latter is the best option for those who rent, as it avoids the need to chase cables behind a wall, while the former is, in truth, the more robust.

If you are substantially refurbishing, you have an opportunity to 'future-proof' any new cabling you install – so it is able to meet not only current requirements but also future demands as technology inevitably advances. Home entertainment is now a highly specialist field, with new developments constantly being made, so it is worthwhile taking advantage of all the free advice many experts offer, so that you can make the best choice for your own specific needs.

The other issue to consider is hardware, from TVs to home computers and hi-fi systems. Again there is a plethora of choice, but there are four criteria that should always be considered:

☐ Always test a product out and never buy sight unseen or sound unlistened to. The better-quality audio suppliers will have acoustically insulated rooms on their premises for just this purpose, and will be able to advise on the best capacity and positioning of equipment such as speakers.

☐ As with furniture, always measure your hardware in relation to the available space. You may crave an enormous television screen, but you may not have room to accommodate it comfortably, or even to watch it. Recommended viewing distances vary considerably, but a good rule of thumb is between two and five times the width of the screen (remember screens are commonly referred to by measurements, in inches, on the diagonal, not the width).

☐ Unless you want your home to look like an electronics store, most technology is best concealed. Admittedly some manufacturers do take great care with aesthetics, so it is up to you how you harmonize the 'lookers' with the rest of your decorative scheme (see Eclectic, page 68). But if harmonizing is not an option, then concealment is your only recourse. In this case allow for the additional circulation space necessary for ventilation. Your supplier will be able to advise you what the minimum should be.

☐ Provenance, running costs and afterlife should always be considered when purchasing home-entertainment equipment (or anything for that matter), including personal computers. The manufacture of gaming stations, televisions, computers and audio equipment often employs hazardous heavy metals and brominated fire-retardants (see page 166), though legislation in many developed countries is changing to demand less environmentally harmful manufacturing processes.

Some notes on televisions

Investing in a new television is particularly fraught with 'options', not merely framed by price. A dip into the internet is likely to make you want to take up a nice hobby instead. In the end, a combination of preferred screen size, set size, picture quality, final position and budget will determine your choice of technology.

To test picture quality, play a DVD featuring dimly lit scenes. You should be able to do this in store. By doing this, you can judge the all-important clarity of black, which is a good indicator of overall performance.

The ideal height of a screen is when the middle is at eye level when you are seated. If this is not possible, then an adjustable bracket can be used, though brackets are not pretty and should not be permanently exposed.

Viewing range – which is a different concept to viewing distance and means the greatest angle from which you can still read a screen without distortion – can vary with different technologies at different sizes. It therefore will relate specifically to the shape of the space for which your television is destined.

If you are wanting also to use your television screen for computer gaming, ensure that it features the appropriate cable sockets. You may also want to put some extra thought into its location.

Standard LCD (liquid crystal display) televisions use half as much power as CRT (cathode ray tube) televisions. Plasma screen televisions use around four times as much as CRT televisions.

Standby modes mean that electrical equipment, including multi-room systems that require the central 'hub' to be constantly powered, will continue to gorge on electricity even when it is not in use. Therefore, equipment with an 'off' button, as well as a 'sleep' mode, will be less costly to run, not to mention less greedy.

An integrated digital television (IDTV) is considered more energy-efficient than a digital TV with separate set-top box. This is not only because of the self-evident efficiencies of using one machine instead of two, but also because IDTVs can usually be switched off at the mains without any loss of programming data. Equipment is sometimes labelled to indicate optimum energy performance.

SECURITY

It is a sad fact of life that our homes must be protected from intruders. Fitting lights with timers is a low-tech way of giving the illusion that someone is home, and on guard. Automated systems can be programmed to turn lights on and off, open and close blinds and curtains, and probably imitate a pack of Dobermans. Choice will be determined by what you have to protect, where you live and your budget.

Movement-activated outdoor lighting has always been popular but can be inefficient and can disturb neighbours. An alternative solution is to install permanent low-intensity decorative lighting that will illuminate dark corners.

If you need a safe, the best thing to do is to keep it permanently concealed. If you are having any kind of built-in cabinetry installed, such as a wardrobe, a section with a false back or floor will act as a fairly effective disguise.

Alarm systems require electrical power, meaning that cables will usually need to be chased into walls and floors, though some sensors can be wireless. Requirements should be incorporated into any overall electrical plan prior to the commencement of construction.

If window grilles are considered necessary, the most imaginative thing to do is commission a metalwork artist to convert what can resemble prison bars into something attractively sculptural. Shutters constitute another effective obstacle to uninvited entry, though they do not allow daylight to penetrate in quite the same way.

8

doing it yourself

8

doing it yourself

After nearly every public holiday, especially the ones in the spring, the news will feature an item about some luckless do-it-yourselfer who has encountered calamity, usually darkly hilarious, at least to my schoolgirl sense of humour. A story I remember well is where someone cut through the beams in their roof to convert their attic into living space – the roof fell in. But doing it yourself need not end in tears, or in extra expense to put things right. You just need to be realistic about your skills, take your time and follow the rules.

Or not. Because there is another way to 'do it yourself', and this is the world of craft, where your home is not just a blank canvas, but an entire artist's studio. Here the only rules that need apply are the rules of creativity, of which there are none.

You may never have contemplated making things for your own home, but home-style handicraft has a well-established precedent (think cave painting). It is thrifty, can be deeply satisfying and therapeutic, and is now, apparently, 'cool'.

If done well, 'doing it yourself' can save you money as well as make your home uniquely personal.

PAINTING

Basic ingredients

- [ ] ladder
- [ ] filling knife
- [ ] sandpaper – a variety of grades from rough to smooth plus wet-and-dry
- [ ] sanding block (a rectangular piece of wood you can wrap sandpaper around)
- [ ] lint-free rags
- [ ] masking tape
- [ ] new or laundered dustsheets
- [ ] old knife (to open cans of paint)
- [ ] scraper
- [ ] 30cm- (12in-) lengths of wooden dowel (to stir or mix up paint)
- [ ] sugar soap or regular detergent (to clean surfaces before painting)
- [ ] large decorator's sponges (to clean surfaces before painting)
- [ ] recycled glass jars (to clean brushes)
- [ ] 'painting clothes' or overalls, including a close-fitting hat, such as a baseball cap
- [ ] extra protection – face masks, disposable gloves, eye protection
- [ ] vacuum cleaner (for sucking up all the dust – there will be lots)
- [ ] variety of brushes
- [ ] paint (to estimate how much you need, refer to your intended paint's covering guidelines; remember that darker or brighter colours will require twice as many coats as lighter colours).
- [ ] paint kettles (metal pots with a handle)

Extra ingredients for walls and ceilings

- [ ] all-purpose filler (Spackle)
- [ ] fine filler
- [ ] flexible filler (for joints that may experience movement, such as near a door frame)
- [ ] plasterboard primer if painting fresh plasterboard
- [ ] emulsion (flat latex) paint, to use thinned as a primer for newly plastered walls
- [ ] moulding primer, for any mouldings
- [ ] variety of rollers (including small- and long-handled for behind radiators) or paint pads
- [ ] paint trays
- [ ] extending pole

Extra ingredients for woodwork

- [ ] wood filler
- [ ] wood primer
- [ ] hot-air gun
- [ ] shave hook
- [ ] wire brush
- [ ] knot sealer (for new wood only)
- [ ] sanding sponge (for sanding around mouldings – just rinse out when full of dust, and then reuse)

Extra ingredients for metalwork

- [ ] steel wool
- [ ] metal primer
- [ ] metal paint stripper
- [ ] turpentine or white spirit (mineral spirits)
- [ ] rust killer
- [ ] metal filler

Basic rules

- [ ] Prepare, prepare, prepare. Although you might be gagging to reinvent your home with the transformative power of paint, the more you prepare, the better the finish will be. This will take patience, though, so put on some music, get the kettle on and open a large can – not of paint but of cookies. This is, after all, how the professionals start work.
- [ ] If you are painting an entire room, paint in the following sequence to avoid new paint higher up in a room spoiling that lower down:
  1 — Ceiling
  2 — Walls
  3 — Doors and windows
  4 — Ceiling mouldings
  5 — Skirtings (baseboards)
  6 — Radiators
- [ ] Before beginning to paint anywhere, ensure that everything you do not want covered in paint is protected. Use new or freshly laundered dustsheets to give general cover and masking tape to guarantee clean edges. You yourself will require 'painting clothes' or overalls, and a hat will protect you from attracting uninvited hair colour.
- [ ] Always wipe up any spillages as soon as they occur.
- [ ] Make sure the space in which you paint is well ventilated.

How to paint walls and ceilings

1 — First check that your walls and ceilings are not about to disintegrate. If they need to be replastered, or even covered in fresh plasterboard, it is best to get a specialist in. Plastering is a skilled job. New plaster and plasterboard will need to be primed before being painted. Thinned emulsion (flat latex) can be used on plaster and a specialist primer on plasterboard. If your walls are covered in wallpaper, hire a steamer to help you scrape it away.

2 — On walls that are in fairly good condition, scrape away any loose plaster and vacuum away dust.

3 — Dampen the resulting cavities with a wet paintbrush.

4 — Fill with all-purpose filler (Spackle). Larger cavities may take several layers that will each need to dry before the next layer is applied. Really large cavities can be filled with screwed-up newspaper and then filled.

5 — Sand down dry filler to a smooth finish using your sandpaper.

6 — Wash down walls using sugar soap or detergent and sponges.

7 — If your walls and ceilings are going to be different colours, you will need to 'cut in', that is, using one of your brushes, carefully paint in the perimeter of the allotted colour.

8 — You are now ready to fill in between the lines. A roller can cover a lot of surface area very quickly but can give an orange-peel effect, which is not always welcome. A good compromise between speed and finish is a painting pad. Both pads and rollers can be fitted to extension poles in order to paint ceilings. Brushes are traditional but time-consuming (and backbreaking on ceilings) and require particular skill to get a seamless finish. To use a roller or pad, you will need to decant paint into one of your trays; to use brushes, decant paint into a paint kettle.

9 — Allow each coat to dry completely before applying another – and do not be alarmed if when you first apply paint it looks nothing like it did on the paint chart. It will once it dries.

10 — To paint behind radiators, use a special long-handled small roller.

11 — When you are ready to paint any mouldings, be sure that they are cleaned and primed first, and then use your finest paintbrushes and a steady hand.

How to paint woodwork

1 — If existing paintwork is in good condition, wash with detergent first and then lightly sand to create a key (rough surface) so the new paint will stick. Vacuum and wash again to remove all the dust.

2 — For paintwork in worse condition – blistered, flaking or multilayered – you need to remove all paint to bare wood. Do this using a combination of a hot-air gun, a wire brush and a shave hook, for removing paint out of mouldings. (Chemical strippers can be used but are highly toxic.) If using a hot-air gun, keep it moving so that it does not scorch the wood. The paint you remove will be very hot, so use something like an old baking tray to catch the detritus and wait until it is completely cool before disposing of it. If using a hot-air gun on windows, ensure that you have fitted the protective

metal attachment (a heat deflector) that will stop the heat from cracking the window glass.

3 — If there are any chips that need filling, apply a primer, then the wood filler, and then sand to a smooth finish. For large areas that require sanding use a power tool, such as an orbital sander.

4 — For new timber, apply knot sealer to the knots and then a coat of primer, filling and sanding back as necessary.

5 — For smaller areas, such as skirting boards (baseboards) and window frames, apply paint with brushes, working in the direction of the wood's grain.

6 — For larger areas, such as doors, apply the paint first in the direction of the grain and then feather in across the grain to get an even finish, completing with strokes back in the direction of the grain. This will avoid the appearance of brush strokes.

7 — Paint panelled doors in a tried and tested sequence (see diagram).

8 — For flush doors, mentally divide the width in half and the length in thirds or quarters. Begin with the top left-hand section, moving on to the top right-hand section, then to the left-hand section below, and so on, until the door is painted.

9 — For doors with different colours, or even patterns, on each side, there is the matter of which of those two finishes to apply to the edge of the door and architrave (the moulding around the door). On doors, if there is no intumescent strip (which divides the door), go for the colour facing into a room rather than out to a corridor or passageway. The same principle should be applied to architraves.

10 — Paint sash (double-hung) windows in a tried and tested sequence (see diagram).

11 — For casement windows, prop the window open when you paint. This way, there is no danger of it being sealed shut when the paint dries.

How to paint metal

1 — To paint a radiator, first make sure it is turned off and is cold. Wash it using detergent and a sponge. Give the surface a key using wet-and-dry sandpaper.

2 — Apply paint to both the radiator and the pipes, protecting valves with masking

tape. A handy piece of cardboard slipped behind a pipe as you paint it will protect the surrounding area from stray brush strokes.

3 — Use the same method for metal window frames that are in relatively good condition.

4 — If metal windows are in poor condition, wear eye protection while you use a wire brush to remove loose paint and rust. Scrub well with detergent and rinse. Wipe down with turpentine or white spirit (mineral spirits). When dry, paint with rust killer and fill any crevices with metal filler. When this is dry, sand down. A metal primer will give an extra-smooth finish. Apply paint.

How to apply paint effects to walls

Paint effects can look heavenly or hideous – there is simply no middle ground. For this reason it is worth trying out ideas on a separate piece of board. In a sense, a paint effect is whatever you choose it to be, depending on colour and application, but there are some well-established recipes that can be a good starting point.

Colourwashing

This effect is suitable for imperfect walls.

1 — Select a choice of water-based paints, such as a pale base coat plus a lighter and/or darker colour. The number of colours you choose is up to you. Paint the wall in your chosen base colour and allow to dry.

2 — Make up a wash by thinning down the accompanying coloured paint – approximately 1 part paint to at least 4 parts water. Apply the wash one colour at a time with a large, soft brush or lint-free cloth.

Glazing

This effect is also especially suitable for imperfect walls.

1 — Paint walls with your chosen oil- or water-based paint. Oil-based paint will give a richer, more substantial finish, and water-based paint a more ethereal effect.

2 — Apply a glaze (sometimes called scumble glaze) in a slightly darker shade, either in the same or a contrasting hue. Note that a water-based glaze can only be used over a water-based paint.

Dry brushing

This effect will look its best on perfect walls.

1 — Paint the wall with a water-based paint.

2 — Select another water-based paint in a different colour or shade. Dip a hard, wide brush into this second paint colour and remove as much excess paint as is reasonable. You want the brush to be 'dry'. Apply your barely laden paintbrush to the wall in cross-hatched strokes.

3 — Repeat for more intensity, and finish with a matte varnish for extra protection.

Sponging, ragging, bagging, dragging and stippling

All these effects will look their best on perfect, as opposed to imperfect, walls. They all use the same mix of ingredients but different application methods.

1 — In all cases paint your wall in either a water- or oil-based paint. Oil-based paint will generally look classier and take longer to dry, and can be easier to use over a large surface area. For dragging, oil-based paint is recommended.

2 — Select a contrasting paint and dilute 1 part paint to 4 parts dissolving liquid. For water-based paints dilute with water or a water-based glaze for a bit of gloss. For oil-based paints dilute with turpentine or white spirit (mineral spirits), or try oil-based glaze for that same touch of gloss.

3 — For sponging, dip a sponge in your contrasting diluted paint. Remove the excess and apply to the wall. An alternative technique is to paint your contrasting diluted paint on the wall and then sponge it off with a clean sponge. To be honest, there is not much difference between the two.

4 — Ragging (and ragging off) is exactly the same, but you use a scrunched-up rag instead of a sponge. Ditto bagging (and bagging off), where you use a scrunched-up plastic bag containing a rag.

5 — For dragging, you will need a brush called a flogger. To create this effect, paint your contrasting paint mixture onto the wall in the regular way, then apply your flogger to the top of the wall and pull it down, with an extraordinarily steady hand, to the bottom. Repeat. Owing to the precision required, this is best executed using an oil-based finish, and when sober.

6 — Stippling requires a stippling brush, or any kind of firm-bristled hand-brush. Dip this into your contrasting diluted paint, remove the excess and stipple the wall with a dabbing action. A chic elaboration of stippling is to go very dark, using a family of slightly different hues, each applied in separate layers. When all is dry, rub all over with a mixture of artist's oil paint in raw umber diluted in an oil-based glaze.

7 — The addition of a matte varnish will give your finished surface extra protection.

Stencilling

The only way this effect is ever going to work is if you take inspiration from the graffiti artists Banksy or Blek le Rat.

1 — Draw your design on thin card (posterboard). Using a scalpel with a 10A blade, cut out your design.

2 — Tape your stencil to the intended surface and then carefully apply spray paint or paint loaded onto a stiff brush. Watch out for the stencil lifting, as this will smudge the edges, and be sure to protect the area surrounding your stencil, too.

Stripes

A striped wall can look candy-cane sweet or informally tailored. Either carefully mask each stripe from the other using low-tack masking tape or, for a more freestyle look, tie elastic bands around a foam roller and use the roller in the usual manner. If you have a fairly steady hand, stripes painted freehand over faint pencil lines can look good – the slight wobbliness is part of the effect.

How to apply paint effects to woodwork
Most of the effects that can be applied to walls (see pages 256–7) can be applied to woodwork, too. In addition, there are the effects of craquelure, wax resist and liming – plus any you just make up yourself.

Craquelure
This requires the application of a special crackle glaze. First apply a base coat of paint and then apply the two different coats of the crackle glaze. As they dry, the finish will crack to emulate 'age'.

Wax resist
A thin coat of wax applied to painted woodwork before painting with a contrasting colour will create a 'resist', which when rubbed off with a cloth will expose the paint colour below.
1 — Paint with your base colour first, if any.
2 — Rub over with a white wax candle.
3 — Paint over with your chosen colour. When the paint is dry, rub with a soft cloth.

Liming (pickling)
Limed (pickled) wood has had a coat of liming (pickling) paste or wax worked into bare, open-grained wood, such as oak or ash, using a brush. The paste or wax is then rubbed off using a clean, dry rag to create a washed-out, beachside look. A close-grained wood, such as pine, can also be used, but it will need a good old going-over with a stiff wire brush, so it is best to do this when you need to let off some steam.

Staining
Staining gives timber a transparent colour, and can make less expensive woods look like more luxurious counterparts, though do be sure to buy a very good-quality stain and follow the manufacturer's instructions to the letter. Also apply in cool conditions, as heat will make the stain dry too quickly, before you have had a chance to even it out across the entire surface. Dark, smokey colours will always look smarter than any stain with red tones.

How to paint furniture
However you might paint your furniture, whether it is made from wood or metal, take care not to 'glue' furniture to newspaper, or a dustsheet below, with fresh paint. For wood furniture, knock a small nail into the bottom of each of the legs on which they can safely rest. Once the paint is dry, remove the nails. For metal furniture, a sticky foam pad cut to a size smaller than that of the feet will work in the same way.

Spattering
If you are in a Jackson Pollock kind of a mood, then this is for you. Perfect walls give a good contrast to the imperfect finish, and will make it look like you meant it.
1 — Take extra care protecting those surfaces you do not want painted.
2 — Paint your walls.
3 — Now flick a brush full of a contrasting paint colour at the painted walls. Choose as many colours as you like, but keep to all water-based paints or all oil-based paints.

WALLPAPERING

Ingredients
□ ladder
□ measuring tape
□ spirit level
□ pencil
□ pasting table
□ wallpaper scissors
□ wallpaper paste (if not ready-pasted)
□ paste brush
□ wallpaper brush
□ bucket
□ seam roller
□ scalpel
□ string
□ wallpaper

How to wallpaper
1 — Prepare the wall as you would if you were going to paint it (see page 255, steps 1–6).
2 — For walls in a particularly bad way, instead of replastering or plasterboarding, you can apply lining paper horizontally to the wall.
3 — To apply the wallpaper itself, begin at the focal point of a room and work outward. Measure the length you require and add 5–10cm (2–4in) at the top and the bottom.
4 — Lay the wallpaper face down on the pasting table and roll out the required length. If the paper curls up, tie a piece of string between the table legs at one end and slip the paper between the gap.
5 — With a pasting brush, apply paste to the paper and slide it up the table as you work down the paper, carefully folding the

pasted paper onto itself. Leave for five minutes so the paste can soak in. If you are using a paper with a small repeat pattern and no drop match, then continue with pasting the second piece. If not, don't.

6 — Now, using your spirit level, measure out vertical guidelines left and right for this first piece of paper and mark with a pencil. Once the first piece is ready, fit to the wall following the guidelines. Using the wallpaper brush to brush from the centre outward, brush out bubbles and brush into the junction with the ceiling, or cornice (cove), at the top and the skirting (baseboard) below.

7 — Using your wallpaper scissors, lightly mark a cutting line at the top and bottom. Pull away the top and bottom a little and carefully cut away the excess paper, then brush the edges back onto the wall.

8 — Continue in this way around the room. For large patterns and drop matches, you will need to measure the relationship of the pattern on the paper to its required position on the wall before you cut additional lengths.

9 — To paper around obstacles such as a light switch, turn off the electricity at the mains supply and unscrew the light switch plate so it is just loosened. Paste the length of paper to the top of the light switch plate or obstacle, as for a skirting (baseboard). Using the scalpel, cut a small cross in the paper resting above the obstacle, stopping just short of the corners. Push the paper down around the edges of the obstacle, and cut away the surplus. For a light switch,

tuck the paper behind before tightening the plate.

10 — To paper into window recesses, cut (very carefully) a horizontal line into drops that creep over a window in line with the top of the window recess. Paste the section below that cut line onto the vertical surface at the side of the recess. Then cut a section of paper to fit the horizontal underside with some overlap to run out and vertically up the wall above. Paste the overlap beneath the main drop.

Wallpaper with a difference

The paper you choose to apply to your walls need not be wallpaper, but can be applied using the same ingredients. Try maps, old newspapers, layers of tissue paper or magazine cuttings, and then seal with varnish. You can even apply fabric to a wall with paste. Your imagination is your only limit, but do test the material out first on a separate piece of board.

You could also try decoupage, where images printed on paper or, more unconventionally, fabric, are pasted with layers of white glue. Decoupage is a technique that adapts well to furniture, as the components are small enough to be pasted around curves and corners. Finish with a coat of matte varnish.

And however you treat a wall can be applied to the ceiling, too.

SOFT FURNISHINGS

Creating your own soft furnishings can be one of the most inexpensive ways of refreshing a space, and it is not difficult. You do not even need a sewing machine, though this can save time. The essentials are needles, thread and an iron and ironing board, plus the fabric and any fastenings and trimmings you like. How to make soft furnishings yourself is a huge subject, however, and there is simply not space here to do it justice. There are plenty of good books and websites around, though, packed full of hints, tips and even patterns – and the ones on websites are free.

If you are sewing for the first time, approach soft furnishings in the way a couturier approaches couture, for this is what soft furnishings are, in a way – unique fabric pieces for your home – and first make a 'toile', or a version in an inexpensive fabric, such as a lightweight canvas or cotton. This way, you can afford to make some mistakes, and apply the lessons you learn to the final items.

When choosing fabrics, bear in mind the laundering instructions, so you can decide whether you want to commit to dry-cleaning or not.

Also consider that in the home it is perfectly acceptable to use dress fabrics as well as those designed specifically for upholstery – you just need to use your common sense when it comes to durability.

REFINISHING FLOORS

Ingredients for refinishing a concrete floor
- ☐ floor paint
- ☐ variety of brushes
- ☐ turpentine
- ☐ recycled glass jars
- ☐ paper, tracing paper, pencil
- ☐ scale rule
- ☐ tape measure

How to refinish a concrete floor
If you have ugly concrete floors (not nice, polished concrete ones), treat the problem as an opportunity for colour and pattern, and paint them. Use special, hardwearing floor paint and start in the farthest corner. If you want to include a pattern, first draw a scale plan of the floor and on this develop your design. When complete, draw a measured grid over the top so it can be scaled back up to 1:1 so that your design can then be transferred to the floor with ease.

1 — First ensure your floor is scrupulously clean, by careful vacuuming, washing and drying the floor.

2 — Once your floor is dry, apply your paint, beginning with the corner farthest from the room's entry. You can use a roller, brushes or rags, as your design requires, just ensure you have protected the adjacent walls with paper and masking tape.

3 — Apply at least two coats of paint for durability and be prepared to repaint as time progresses, depending on how much traffic the floor experiences and what your tolerance is for wear and tear.

4 — One way to embrace 'wear and tear' is to paint one colour beneath a contrasting colour over the top, so that as the top colour wears away your floor develops its own decorative effect.

Ingredients for refinishing a wood floor
- ☐ brads (tapered nails with small heads)
- ☐ claw hammer
- ☐ nail punch
- ☐ spare boards
- ☐ crosscut saw
- ☐ chisel
- ☐ sandpaper or sanding machine with attachments
- ☐ plastic dustsheets and tape
- ☐ vacuum cleaner
- ☐ turpentine or white spirit (mineral spirits)
- ☐ lint-free cloths

How to refinish a wood floor
The only other floor that can be easily refinished by the do-it-yourselfer is a solid, nailed wood floor, such as floorboards. As with walls, it is worth preparing floorboards before refinishing them, because this will give the best result. If your floors were previously waxed, you will need to remove this with lots of hot, soapy water before you sand.

1 — Nail down any loose boards with a special nail called a brad, tapping each with a nail punch to make sure the heads sink just below the surface of the board.

2 — Replace any damaged boards by lifting them carefully with a chisel and claw hammer, first at the end and then along the sides so the board does not snap in two. If you want to replace just a section of a board, use a strip of wood to wedge the loosened, damaged piece up off floor level while you use a crosscut saw to remove the damaged part. Cut the new board to size, making sure it is the same thickness as the old, and nail it into place as above.

3 — The next stage is sanding. If your boards are in fairly good condition, and you are planning on painting them, you may be able to get away with a good scrubbing and a light sand, to create a key.

4 — If they are looking a bit rough and/or you want a transparent finish, you will need to hire sanding machines to do a more substantial job. This will create a sandstorm of dust, so seal everything behind plastic sheeting, and even seal up doors before you fire up.

5 — Begin by sanding adjacent strips on the diagonal and then run over the floor in strips in the direction of the boards. Sand the edges with an edge sander. Thin cardboard taped over skirting (baseboards) and the bottoms of architraves (door mouldings) can give added protection.

6 — When you are finished, vacuum thoroughly and wipe down with turpentine or white spirit (mineral spirits). Meanwhile, think about your chosen finish.

7 — Your boards are now ready to be refinished. Paint, including stencilling, is one way to go, but you could also use stain, wood bleach, varnish or liming (pickling) paste or wax. Just follow the manufacturer's instructions and test on a spare board, or on a section that will be covered by furniture, before you apply to your entire floor.

NEW WOOD FLOORS

Ingredients for laying a new wood floor
□ plywood sheets
□ screws
□ underlay
□ plastic sheeting
□ wood glue
□ softwood board, for false skirting
  (baseboards)
□ tongue-and-groove flooring packs
□ crosscut saw

How to lay a new wood floor
In the spirit of being realistic about
your DIY skill set, a tongue-and-groove
suspended wood flooring system is the only
type of wood flooring that should be tackled
by the amateur. Anything else really needs
the professionals, including the installation
of any kind of flooring you wish to have laid
on the diagonal.

1 — First check the condition of your floor.
If it is more then 3mm (¹/8in) out of level,
you will need to fit a plywood subfloor. Saw
the sheets to size and screw them down. If
fitting the floor over concrete, you will also
need to lay a sheet of plastic.

2 — Cover the floor with underlay and begin
to lay your floor.

3 — Most flooring comes with perimeter
wedges and a tamping block. The wedges
are to be placed at the outer edge of the
room to create an expansion gap for
the floor.

4 — The boards at the outer edges should
be laid so that the groove is facing the wall.
Begin by laying the boards short end to
short end along the longest, straightest
wall you have.

5 — Use the cutoff from the last piece you
lay to begin the second row of flooring, so
that the joins in your finished floor are
not aligned.

6 — Some systems will require glue, some
will not. Apply as required and use the
tamping block to make sure subsequent
boards are 'driven home'.

7 — Ideally, flooring should be fitted
beneath a skirting (baseboard). If this is not
possible, do not fit a mean little wood strip
over the expansion gap – it will look cheap.
Instead, make a false skirting out of a wide
strip of board and glue and nail this to the
existing skirting, where it will simply add
more detail. Fill and decorate.

TILES

Stone and slate tiles, as I once learned to
my cost, are best installed by a professional
tiler, but ceramic tiles are a much more
realistic proposition on walls and floors.
Follow this method for your own mosaic
designs, too. Never paint tiles – it will look
terrible. If you want to refresh tiles, either
tile over them or remove them with a chisel
and hammer, and then start again. It will
be worth it.

Ingredients for tiling
□ plywood sheets
□ screws
□ pencil
□ string
□ spirit level
□ adhesive
□ notched spreader
□ trowel
□ flexible filling knife
□ sponges
□ lint-free cloths
□ bucket
□ grout
□ tile spacers
□ tile cutter
□ tile nibbler
□ softwood strips
□ chisel
□ hammer
□ ladder
□ tiles

TILES

How to tile:

Floors

Use a flexible adhesive on a flexible floor – anything that is not concrete or tile. And if you are tiling in a bathrooms or kitchen, use a waterproof adhesive.

1 — Tiles can be laid directly onto concrete subfloors, or even over existing tiles, so long as there is no more than a 3mm ($\frac{1}{8}$in) variation, in which case a plywood subfloor will need to be laid first. If laying tiles over floorboards, you will always need to a fit a plywood subfloor (see page 263, step 1).

2 — Next, draw lines on the floor to divide it in half vertically and then horizontally to create four equal quarters. You need to begin laying tiles in the corner farthest from the exit.

3 — Begin by dry laying a horizontal row of tiles from the central point out to one of the edges of the room. Then dry lay a vertical row of tiles from the last whole tile on the horizontal row into the corner above. The last whole tile you dry lay will be the first tile you lay for real. Mark its position with pencil.

4 — Cut battens the length of four tiles, or four sheets of tiles. Screw down into the floor two of the battens between the two adjacent walls and the first tile. Screw down the two remaining battens to create a square. These are your tiling guides. Fill the gap with adhesive and begin to lay tiles using spacers (which are designed to be left in the adhesive) and a spirit level. Remove the tiling guides and refit so that you can lay down the next set of 16 tiles.

5 — Once the floor has set, usually after about 24 hours, you can fit the edging tiles, which you will need to measure and cut with a tile cutter.

6 — When these have set, apply your grout. Take your time and work on small sections sequentially. After about 15 minutes thoroughly wipe off the excess grout before you move on to the next section, because grout is almost impossible to remove once hard. When all the grout is hardened off, polish the tiles with a soft cloth.

Walls

So long as the surface to be tiled is clean, dry and dust-free, no preparation will be required: the adhesive will make any necessary adjustments for variation in level.

1 — First decide how best to lay out the tiles. For a single wall, it is best to start from a central point and work outward. If tiling something like a shower stall, it is better to start from the outside and work in.

2 — As with all tiling, work in small patches. Apply the adhesive with a notched spreader and press your tiles with spacers onto the surface. Use a tile cutter to cut any straight sections of tile and a tile nibbler to shape tiles around obstructions (it can be helpful to make a paper template first).

3 — When the adhesive is set, fill the lines with grout. Wipe off any excess grout with a damp sponge.

IT'S PERSONAL

The advent of small-batch digital printing has added to the many ways in which it is possible to personalize the materials we use in our homes. Fabric, paper and ceramic tile are particularly suitable applications for this technique. Fabrics can, of course, also be dyed, painted, embroidered, stitched with needlepoint, beaded or appliquéd, while knitting and crochet mean you can make your own 'fabrics' almost from scratch.

Painting need not consist of a single block of colour – murals are much more personal. In the absence of practised accuracy, pursue the expressive and consider not only walls or floors, but also doors, fireplaces, table tops and even the bath. If you are nervous about applying your flights of fancy directly to surfaces, test them out at scale on paper and board first.

NEW SKILLS

Creating a home is an opportunity to reveal innate creativity. It can also offer a chance to develop that creativity by taking courses in pottery, printmaking, glassblowing, carpentry, fine art and metalwork. You may be surprised to discover just how talented you are, all to the benefit of your home – and your life.

9

shopping

9
shopping

There are those who love shopping and those who do not. Either way, it is a very necessary process to creating a home and can be made more enjoyable by planning first. If you find shopping boring or frustrating, it is a sure sign you are probably buying something that you will find boring to live with, or your criteria are unrealistic.

TOOLS

To shop well you will need tools. The first of these is a simple list that will help you focus on what you really need, just as in grocery shopping.

The second tool you will need is a tape measure, to measure items you have your eye on and the dimensions of their destination. You will also need to measure the widths of doorways and the clearance around any stairs or corners through which your purchases will need to shimmy before coming to rest. Some pieces can be broken down into components to combat tight spots, but do check, and if this is the case either you or someone you hire will need to be on hand to disassemble and reassemble.

I also always carry around samples of the other components in a space to be sure of compatibility. Photographs and scale plans can be similarly useful.

SPENDING

It is easy to think that money is the key to shopping well but, as in most things, 'it's not what you do, it's the way that you do it'.

Just as a chain-store frock can be elevated with luxurious accessories, the same can occur with homes. For example, a dining area can be kitted out with rather ordinary but perfectly serviceable furniture and then dramatized with a breathtaking pendant light by a new, young designer. And the difficult-to-find piece discovered in a garage sale might be inexpensive but far more covetable – and enjoyable to source – than an equivalent mass-produced or costly 'designer' offering from one of the big stores.

Do not ever, though, sacrifice quality on the altar of budget, for it will doubtless cost you more in the long run. When it comes to the essentials, like beds and sofas, spend as much as you can afford, and then be patient until your purse is ready to fill in the gaps.

To help you budget, add a column to your shopping list – when you see something you think might fit the bill, jot down the price. If you do this with all the items on your list before committing to buy anything, you will be giving yourself the space to research less expensive options, as necessary, to keep yourself on budget.

QUANTITIES

Sizes are one thing, quantities are another.

Wallpaper

Wallpaper is perhaps the trickiest item to work out, especially one with a large repeat pattern – more than about 10cm (4in) – or a drop match, where the pattern is dissected vertically by wallpaper edges, or both. I usually let the experts, my decorators, do the math, which you should, too. If you are doing the decorating yourself, just measure the surface area you wish to paper and give the results to your wallpaper supplier to calculate, remembering to deduct windows and doors from the overall area. Roughly about 10 per cent of the total should be added for wastage.

Wallpaper is printed in batches, which means there can be slight variations between rolls from different batches. Make sure that all the wallpaper you need for a room is purchased from the same batch, in which case it is always better to buy too much than not enough.

Paint

The same goes for paint, which should be purchased all at once. Follow the table on the side of the pot to work out how much you need, bearing in mind that dark colours need twice as many coats as light.

Tiles

When buying any kind of tiles, add 10 per cent to the overall quantity to allow for the wastage generated by cutting. Be sure to allow for the different types of tile, such as edge tiles.

Fabrics

The quantity of curtain material you buy should be dictated by height, including an allowance for hems and tabs, and width. As explained on page 217, width should be at least twice that of the window or the breadth of the final curtain, which may, of course, be much wider.

If you are buying fabric for upholstery, always let your upholsterer advise you of how much you need. Never try to work it out yourself, unless you are calculating for a simple pillow.

Worktops

Any worktops or other, similar fixtures you are buying should always be measured up by the supplier. Your attendance at the same time will avoid any misunderstandings about final fit and detail.

Unless you are doing the building work yourself, you should not really need to concern yourself with the quantities of any other kind of finish or fixture. This is what suppliers and contractors are experienced at calculating.

THE SHOPS

You are now ready to shop. The internet is a good place to start, at least to begin with. Here you will be able to research every kind of market, from the mass-produced to the antique and vintage.

If you are buying new, never buy on the internet without first inspecting the goods in the flesh. This may require some sneaky peeks at a competitor's showroom, in which case tell them if you have found the same model on the internet for less, and see if they will at least match the price. If prior inspection is not possible, always confirm what the returns policy is and any follow-up you may need, such as a maintenance programme or guarantee.

Town-centre shops, chain stores at the mall and out-of-town superstores can all be convenient, but they will be convenient for millions of other people, too, so do not be surprised if your home, fitted out in a majority of items from these outlets, looks somewhat bland. The temptation of goods from these stores is also one of price, but there are other ways to secure budget-friendly prices, often with more imaginative results.

I always used to find auctions terrifying until I made my first purchase – a Georgian armchair I bought when I was first married – and realized what an adrenalin rush they can be, as well as a surprisingly rich seam of bargains. The same goes for all other kinds of sales, such as garage sales, yard sales, jumble sales, rummage sales, swap meets or flea markets.

In a world of waste it is well worth checking the internet for recycling programmes, where one person's trash can be another's treasure. I have found some wonderful things at my local municipal dump – it can be surprising what people throw away.

At the other end of the spectrum are 'designer' goods, a term that always makes me smirk. Everything man-made has to go through a process of design, to decide what goes where, or it could not be made. On this basis everything is 'designer'. What 'designer' really means in this context is 'signature', and often the input of the personality involved is limited to just that.

What is really important is not the name that is being exploited to push up sales, but whether you feel the piece in question has design integrity in and of itself. If it has, then you should buy it, with or without the 'name'.

Exhibitions and shows

Graduate shows feature work by the up-and-coming generation of design talent, full of fresh, individual ideas at affordable prices. The other great sources of great design, and designers, are design shows and exhibitions. These are mostly held for the trade, but some hold a public day. And sometimes the larger trade fairs will generate satellite consumer fairs and events.

GOING BESPOKE

If you do not find exactly what you are after, then you will need to go bespoke, and a design show is a good place to find a designer/maker. Also try relevant guilds, institutions and galleries.

The advantage of bespoke (custom) pieces is that not only are they designed specifically for you and the space in which you live, but also no one else will have exactly what you have. You may be surprised how affordable commissioned pieces can be, comparable to equivalent ready-made pieces in the mid- to upper end of the market.

When it comes to makers it is a buyer's market, so take time to do your research, including visiting workshops and inspecting previous work in situ, if possible. Once you have appointed someone you would like to work with, ensure that all terms of business are confirmed in writing, including a detailed brief, budget and time frame, so there are no surprises for either party. Expect to pay a deposit before you see any designs, with the balance to be paid as the piece is manufactured and/or on delivery. And if you are unsure of anything being proposed to you, or need to see more samples, speak up. The best designer/makers will value a full and thorough exchange of thoughts and ideas, which will be all to the good of the final piece.

THE TRADE

Trade showrooms are usually the preserve of professional designers and decorators. This is because trade suppliers are geared to service trade buyers – not consumers, with all their questions. It is also because it was once standard in the world of the semi-aristocratic interior designer and decorator that fees would be earned based on the difference between trade and retail. The interior designer would act as a kind of shop front and charge clients retail prices. In this way, they would avoid the embarrassing business of actually charging fees. Thankfully more transparent practices are taking hold.

For a 'layperson' to take a peak inside these showrooms is not against the law. Most showroom managers and their staff will probably be very friendly and helpful, though you may have trouble making a purchase for the reasons above. Showrooms are, unsurprisingly, protective of professional privileges.

TRAVELOGUE

Buying things for your home when travelling abroad can be very seductive, but once installed they can be about as welcome as that bottle of ouzo still lurking in the back of the drinks cabinet. It may have seemed wonderful in the Mediterranean sunshine but seems a bit naff back home. Better to institute a cooling-off period – if you think you have fallen for something, take all the details and, when you get home, if you still think it will work, contact the shop owner and have it shipped over. This is, after all, the world of the internet and next-day shipping. But remember, some of the best souvenirs are ideas.

LIAISON

In some cases you may be purchasing from different suppliers who are working on the same component. For example, you may have bought kitchen cabinets from one outlet and a countertop from another. In this case it is vital that suppliers liaise directly to avoid any oversights. However, you must also insist that you are copied in on all communications so there are no surprises when it comes to details. Or the bill.

DELIVERY AND INSTALLATION

When buying any item that needs to be delivered and/or installed, always check to see if these are included in the price. If not, ask if the supplier can provide these services and if so at what price. Then source comparative quotes so you can get the best deal. Always confirm delivery lead times, too, especially on a larger project where you need to coordinate the installation of different items.

As soon as anything is delivered, check to make sure it is what you expected and contact the supplier immediately if it is not. You cannot expect a supplier to make amends if you do not.

MAINTENANCE AND GUARANTEES

When buying any item, always clarify the degree of guarantee and maintenance advice. You do not want to invest in anything where upkeep will be tiresome.

10

not doing it yourself

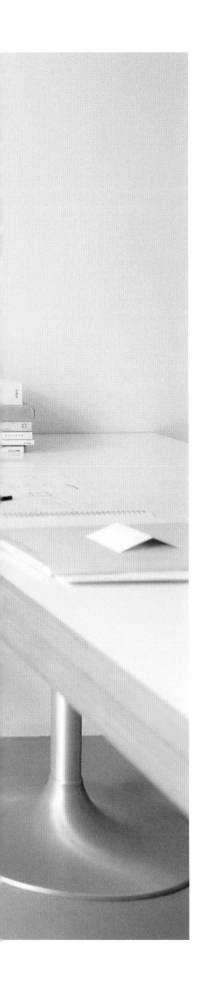

10

not doing it yourself

Once you have worked out your design, it will need to be implemented. And the scale of your plans will determine how you execute your project. If you feel up to it, or are on a super-tight budget, you might take on minor works yourself (see Chapter 8). If not, those minor works can be done by professionals. Larger works will require even more professionals, and of different kinds. This is because building work, and specifically structural work, even on small projects, involves layers of specialist information that needs to be coordinated and efficiently executed, or disaster will ensue. After all, you would not perform your own dental work, would you?

Whatever the scenario, there is one constant: the more time you spend planning your refurbishment, the more control you will have over its realization. This is because you will already have ironed out all the surprises that cost extra time and money – well, at least as many of them as you can possibly hope to. As they say in the military, perfect planning prevents poor performance. Equally, as I have always said in design, there is no such thing as an entirely problem-free refurbishment. But the quality of the people on your team will be judged by how effectively they manage those problems, and that includes you. Hysteria is always a hindrance, not a help.

And remember, any changes made after work has started will always add to the final cost, even if you think you are only exchanging one element for another.

If your refurbishment plans do not include any major structural work, and you can spare the time, you are well placed to manage their implementation yourself.

HOW TO PERFECTLY MANAGE YOUR OWN PROJECT

The management of even minor works can benefit from the methods employed by professionals on larger projects. And in the end these methods are as much a question of common sense as experience.

Managing a project, even a small one, will take time and require attention to detail. The more you approach the process like a job, the better it will be for all parties. Homes are emotional spaces but emotion can only compromise building work, so cool, businesslike, objective detachment is crucial. In this way you will be better able to solve any little (and large) problems as they arise, instead of apportioning blame while the problem atrophies.

I cannot emphasize enough the importance of writing everything down, from those things that you yourself need to do, to all of those you want others to do for you. When it comes to written instructions for others, it is helpful if you specify exactly how you want something done, even down to the way you want window frames painted. That way, those you employ are less likely to use their initiative, which is not always desirable.

The specification

Below is an extract from a specification my own practice has produced for a project:

□ All new plastered surfaces to have 1 no-mist coat and any imperfections to be filled, sanded back and made good prior to main decorations.
□ Any existing ironmongery to be removed prior to painting and fitted after completion of decorations.
□ All existing window frames to be rubbed down, and cracks and holes to be stopped and filled and rubbed down.
□ Any existing window frames that have blistering or flaking paint, burn paint off to bare wood. Rub back to a smooth surface, and prime bare wood ready for eggshell top coat.
□ All new skirtings (baseboards) and architraves to be knotted and primed ready for eggshell top coats.
□ All windowsills to be rubbed down. If blistering and flaking paint is evident, burn off to bare wood. Rub back to a smooth surface, and prime bare wood ready for eggshell top coats.
□ All new door liners to be filled at junctions, rubbed down, knotted and primed prior to eggshell top coats.
□ All ceilings and walls, except for wet areas, to be in matte emulsion (flat latex).
□ Wet areas – allow for ceilings and walls to be painted in eggshell finish.
□ Where dark coloured paint finishes are used on walls, allow for 3–4 top coats.

Not the most gripping read, but it illustrates how you can never have enough detail, no matter how much seems a matter of common sense. Assumptions are where arguments breed and where budgets get out of control.

At the same time, on a minor domestic project run by a lay person, a firm of good repute should not necessarily need the forensic detail of how to execute something, so long as you are both agreed on what the expected outcomes are. These outcomes should still be enshrined in a contract, or a simple letter of appointment, outlining the scope of works, and the rights and responsibilities of you and your contractors, including price and a payment schedule.

The budget

The detailed instructions contained in a specification will help firms who are bidding for work submit accurate costs, too. To budget effectively, consolidate all of the elements in your project, including all services and supplies, on a spreadsheet. As different costs are submitted, add these to the sheet and then add them all up.

If you are over budget, you will need to either negotiate or amend your requirements, or both. Talk to your contractors to see if there are different ways things could be done to reduce cost. Research less costly finishes and fixtures. Or phase the works that you want to do, implementing some now and some at a later date, though this can be more expensive overall.

Most importantly, juggle your budget on paper before you start committing any proportion of it. All building projects should allow for at least a 10 per cent contingency – especially in older buildings, which can be full of surprises from dry rot to ancient wiring. Small jobs should not really need much more than this, so long as you have been clear in your instructions to those who are executing the work, and they themselves are professional and trustworthy.

Contractors and suppliers

To find professional and trustworthy firms a good starting point is word of mouth, but your researches should not end here – inspect previous work and talk to previous clients. Good firms will welcome this as it shows you are taking due responsibility for their potential appointment. And never work with friends or family.

Devise a shortlist of two or three candidates for each job you need doing. Hiring individual subcontractors instead of a main contractor can save you cash, but bear in mind that the extra cost of a main contractor is spent on their expert coordination of subcontractors. This does not stop you influencing the choice of those subcontractors, however, especially in the case of any specialist fittings and fixtures. Any upholstery will always be a separate item.

Invite each firm to meet you at your home and then talk through your list of what needs doing, indicating whether you will be expecting materials to be supplied or not. If you want materials to be supplied, and have a preference, specify exactly what it is that you want – perhaps a certain kind of paint, fabric or light switch? Maybe even 'eco plaster' and PVC-free wiring? Expect them to add a percentage to the price for their time administrating purchase and delivery.

Being 'green' does not end with choice of fixtures and fittings. Construction waste accounts for an alarmingly high percentage of landfill, so work with contractors who have a deliberate policy of minimizing waste in the first place, who recycle as much as possible of the waste they produce and who take extra care over disposing waste that cannot be recycled (though even the odd bit of VOC-containing paint can usually find a home).

Whether you have produced (or even need) your own scale drawings or not, it is at this stage that firms should take measurements, measuring up for flooring, wallpaper, curtains, and so on, so that they can accurately price a job. They may need to produce drawings as part of this process, for example in the case of any joinery item, for which it is only reasonable that a fee be paid, though this will not always be expected.

When inviting firms to bid for a job, also ask them for details of the insurance they hold and their terms and conditions. You need to be sure that anyone working on your home is indemnified against any loss or damage to you, your home, the project itself or any third party that comes into contact with the works – this includes neighbours. You should also alert your own building's insurance company before having any work done and on completion of those works, too. Curtain hanging obviously does not count, but anything to do with plumbing and electricity, or digging into walls, floors and ceilings, does. They may well ask for further details or documents to guarantee cover.

When you have chosen who you want to work with, draft your letter of appointment. This should establish house rules, as appropriate – such as which bathroom can be used, the use of the kettle, working hours

– and confirm not only the works and final quality agreed, but also the frequency and method of payment.

Note that you should never have to pay contractors or subcontractors any money upfront. If they ask you to, think twice about hiring them, as this usually means their cash flow is up the spout. You do not want a contractor to go bankrupt when they have your money but you have little to none of their services. Instead, it is common for payments to be made in stages commensurate to the work completed and two weeks in arrears.

If you are dealing with suppliers yourself, they will probably expect a deposit with your order. You will also need to ensure that their delivery lead times have been factored into your contractor's or subcontractor's programme – you do not want to be paying workers while they wait for materials to arrive.

Supplies should always be inspected as soon as they are delivered. That way, any defects can be reported immediately and remedy made.

Also confirm how long the works will take. Ask firms to give you realistic timescales rather than optimistic ones and then, in the same way that you would augment a budget, add at least a 10 per cent contingency.

Once people are working for you, the best thing to do is let them get on with the job. No one performs well when someone is constantly peering over their shoulder. And always pay on time.

Nevertheless, if you have concerns, raise them rather than letting them fester, but raise them in a businesslike manner and be specific about your complaints or queries. As in any human relationship, people generally reflect our own behaviour back to us. Hostility invites hostility. Treat contractors and suppliers with respect and kindness and it will generally be reciprocated. Of course, there will be the odd exception that proves the rule. If you are unhappy with any work, be clear about why you are unhappy and allow an opportunity for the work to be redone. If you are still not happy, pay for the work that does meet your expectations, and find someone better to finish the job.

Once the works are complete, thank your contractors and suppliers; this rarely happens and they will appreciate it. And enjoy your new home.

The interior decorator
If after reading this you realize you do not have the appetite or time for this kind of work, hire an interior decorator. While you may not require their creative skills, though a sounding board is always useful, their project management skills will be just what you need.

Interior decorators will charge a fee calculated as a percentage of the overall spend or on a time basis. They may also be earning on the difference between the trade price they can secure for supplies and the retail price they charge you. This is standard professional practice, though somewhat oblique. A more transparent arrangement is to pay a fee reflecting the investment of time and expertise and a percentage handling charge on the trade price of supplies to compensate for the time taken to administrate purchase and delivery, not to mention access to trade discounts.

To find the ideal decorator for you, contact trade associations as well as taking personal recommendations. Meet with their previous clients, inspect their previous work and check out their professional indemnity insurance arrangements.

HOW TO BE THE PERFECT CLIENT

On larger projects that involve significant structural changes, you will need expert assistance to translate your ideas into more sophisticated instructions, as the language of building is quite different to that used in everyday life. If you have developed your own design concepts, as the earlier chapters in this book have guided you to do, there are two ways of going about this: working with an interior designer or architect, or working with a surveyor. Within each of these choices you have the further option of engaging a quantity surveyor, who can run the accounts on your project, and a project manager, who can run the building works.

In both cases you must be clear on what the scope of responsibility is. In essence, it will be to ensure that the agreed design is comprehensive and fully resolved, is built within a certain time frame and budget, and complies with all rules and regulations.

The design professional

The home is an intimate space, so designing a new home will necessitate a degree of intimacy with your design professional, whichever kind you choose. Consider this when you are interviewing candidates, which will effectively be like going on a blind date. Think about whether you feel you can fully express yourself with them, and they with you. Communication, as any marriage guidance counsellor will tell you, is the foundation of any good relationship.

As you would with contractors and subcontractors, take references, inspect previous work and talk to previous clients.

Be precise about the services you require and about fees. All design professionals will calculate fees either as a percentage of the contract sum or on a time basis, sometimes both, where some parts of the project will be charged on a percentage basis and some at an hourly rate. All design professionals should also have professional indemnity insurance.

All these details should be put in writing in the form of a Letter of Appointment.

Working with an interior designer or architect

Even if you have a very clear vision of what you want to achieve creatively, you could still engage an interior designer or architect. A good architect should be as accomplished at creating well-finished and sophisticated interior spaces as they are at designing buildings, though some practices will be stronger in certain fields. Likewise, the practice of a good interior designer will be firmly couched in architecture, concerned as much with the arrangement and function of space as the arrangement and function of sofa cushions.

If you want both, then an interior designer will be the better bet, though if you wish to significantly extend your home the services of a good architect, at least in the first instance, will be indispensable.

Whichever type of professional you choose to work with, it will be useful to talk through your creative ideas no matter how fixed you feel they might be, especially with those who are very experienced in rising to

similar challenges. An interior designer or architect will also be able to produce and coordinate all the other work that a building project requires, from construction drawings to liaising with a structural engineer, surveyors, planning authorities and building regulators. They can even advise you on engaging a landscape designer, and coordinate their works, too.

Once this process is concluded, they can produce a tender package. Not a love letter, but a package of scaled construction drawings and a detailed specification against which prices can be submitted.

Your architect or interior designer can then analyse the tender prices and assist you in hiring the best people for the job. Do not select on price alone – your home and your life are far too valuable. Remember to investigate previous projects and talk to previous clients.

The responsibility for ensuring the correct contracts are in place, along with all the appropriate insurances, can also be given to your architect or interior designer. So can the responsibility for administrating that contract – certifying the degree of work done to releasing stage payments and monitoring any variations and omissions to the agreed works.

Toward the end of your project, your architect or interior designer can work with you to draft a snagging list so that any defects can be made good. It is then standard that a period of time should elapse before the final percentage of the sum due to the contractor is paid. This is called the defects period and allows for building work to settle. The length of time is usually six months, at the end of which the contractors will return to make good any further defects. On completion, the final sum is released to them and a completion certificate issued.

Working with a surveyor

Another route is to work with a surveyor. They will not have the artistic training that an architect or interior designer will have had, but they will be experienced and trained in all the other skills you will need.

The Royal Institute of Chartered Surveyors is a good place to look, with offices around the world. There are, however, different kinds of surveyor with different skill sets, so be clear about what you are after when engaging in discussions with firms. Know that surveyors who work on bridges and airports are unlikely to be the most suitable fit for you and your home. A new, young firm, on the other hand, could be ideal and will relish the opportunity.

Quantity surveyors

A quantity surveyor is someone who plays the role of accountant in a building context. They will advise you how fair tendered building costs are and negotiate with contractors as required. It is often thought that this is the job of interior designers and architects, and on smaller projects it usually is, but this is not part of their training. Therefore, on larger projects or ones that are very time-sensitive, a quantity surveyor can be worth his or her weight in gold, or bricks and mortar.

A note on project managers

A project manager need not be the sole preserve of a subcontracted project. On much larger or more complex projects a project manager can be an invaluable check on the main contractor.

COSTS

The tender process, which elicits building prices, involves a shortlist of firms submitting their prices competitively, and the best man or woman winning. An alternative approach is negotiation – here a single tender is sought, saving time, and then negotiated to a fair and realistic price by a quantity surveyor as necessary. A third option is to deconstruct the process entirely, removing the main contractor and replacing them with a project manager and a team of subcontractors, in addition to a quantity surveyor. In this way there is absolute transparency as to where your money is spent, but it does not necessarily mean that your project will cost less and can be much harder work for you.

Sometimes it is difficult to pinpoint exactly what the job requires, especially when it comes to those items below the surface, in which case a 'guestimate' will need to be made and a provisional sum included in the price for the job. The more provisional sums you can anticipate, the less you will be shocked by 'extras' at the end of the project. Nevertheless always add a contingency sum of 10–30 per cent extra.

When budgeting, also allow for any sales taxes. Any cost or fee estimates and proposals will usually be submitted net of tax. In addition, include the cost of any rented accommodation you will need, plus statutory fees, such as those you may need to pay to local authorities to process any planning and building control applications.

DISPUTE RESOLUTION

During the first golden weeks of your project, when you are putting your team together and everyone loves one another, the last thing you want to contemplate is the potential for divorce. But as in all relationships things can go wrong, especially in intense situations, which is what a building site is, especially if that building site is your home, and works have turfed you out into rented accommodation, and there are lots of different people involved who are not communicating as well as they should.

As soon as there is sign of trouble, call the parties together, sit down at the beginning of a working day when everyone is still fresh, and talk through your concerns, calmly and respectfully, confirming them in writing.

If sitting and talking between yourselves does not solve the problem then you will need to call in the services of an objective third party. It may be small comfort but yours will not be the first or last project to fall victim. The well-established and easily accessible structures that exist to resolve conflict in the construction industry are testament to this unarguable fact.

In the UK the Royal Institute of Chartered Surveyors (RICS), the Royal Institute of British Architects (RIBA) and the National Specialist Contractors Council (NSCC) all provide adjudication services, where fees are restricted and the time frame for judgment, too, making this a quick, inexpensive, though no less stressful route. Alternatively, one can take legal action, in the form of arbitration or litigation, both mutually exclusive. The key difference between the two is that arbitration is held in private and judgment is made by specialists in the field. The key similarity is that they are both very expensive.

Legal action should be avoided at all costs, literally, and one way to do this is to take time choosing the people you work with and then communicate effectively with them. Part of this is ensuring that, if you are in a couple, only one of you is the appointed mouthpiece, and that mouthpiece is the better person for the job.

RECORDS

Just as it is wise to keep financial records for around six years, so it is essential to keep records of any refurbishment work you have commissioned. Design professionals and contractors will usually have a degree of duty of care to you for some time after a project's completion, bound by the type of contract you have in place and the laws of the land in which you live. So you do not want to be wrong-footed by not retaining the reams of documentation your project will have inevitably generated.

On a simpler note, retaining the paint schedule will be a godsend when it is time to redecorate, or when you move out and the new occupants are calling you wondering what that divine shade of grey on the living room wall is.

Retaining guarantees, warranties and maintenance instructions goes without saying. Yet it is surprising how many people do not follow maintenance instructions, which can compromise guarantees and warranties.

afterword

A home should never be considered finished: so long as you live, your home lives with you. Remember this when you have worn yourself ragged, running around shops and dealing with suppliers and contractors, only to find that when all is installed it feels like something is missing. There may well be, but in time it will appear, probably when you are least expecting it, rather like true love. True joy.

0
1
2
3
4
5
6
7
8
9
10

notes, sketches, thoughts & doodles

Use this scaled graph and notepaper, and cut out the scale rules, too, to get going on designing your perfect home straightaway.

FEET 1:10

0

1

2

3

4

5

6

7

8

9

10

INCHES 1:1

0

1

2

3

4

5

6

7

8

9

10

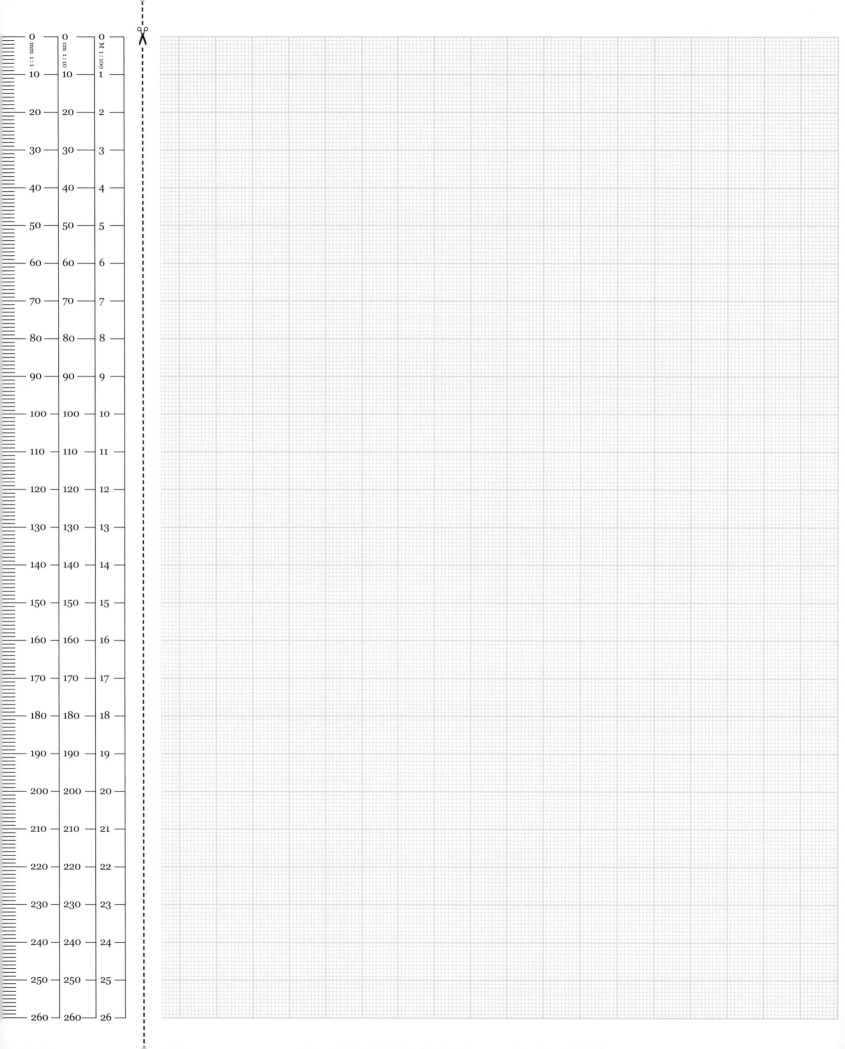

Doodles —

Notes —

suppliers

USEFUL CONTACTS

Better Planet
www.betterplanet.co.uk
*Information on environmentally
sustainable technologies.*

The Building Centre
www.thebuildingcentre.co.uk
*A comprehensive resource of building
materials and techniques.*

Energy Saving Trust UK
www.energysavingtrust.org.uk
*Practical advice and support on saving
energy in the home.*

The Federation of Master Builders
www.fmb.org.uk
A list of reliable and skilled contractors.

The Forestry Stewardship Council
www.fsc.org
*Lists of suppliers of FSC-certified timber
products around the world.*

Green Depot
www.greendepot.com
Sustainable building products in USA.

**The Royal Institute of Chartered
Surveyors**
www.rics.org
A listing of members around the world.

The Wood Window Alliance
www.woodwindowalliance.com

INSPIRATION

100% Design – London
www.100percentdesign.co.uk
Annual design trade show with a public day.

**Cooper-Hewitt, National Design
Museum, New York**
cooperhewitt.org
Watch out for the new RE:DESIGN galleries.

Design Museum London
www.designmuseum.org

Geffrye Museum London
www.geffrye-museum.org.uk
Dedicated to domestic design.

**International Contemporary
Furniture Fair**
www.icff.com
Annual design trade show in New York City.

The Museum of Modern Art (MoMA)
www.moma.org

The School of Life
www.theschooloflife.com
A kind of supermarket for the soul.

Selvedge magazine
www.selvedge.org
Magazine where craft is cool and compelling.

Tent London
www.tentlondon.co.uk
Runs concurrently with 100% Design.

SUPPLIES

Electrical and Lighting

A Shade Above
www.ashadeabove.co.uk
*Will make lamp shades to your design at very
reasonable prices and ship around the world.*

Aldo Bernardi
www.aldobernardi.it
Beautiful electrical fittings from Italy.

Bromleighs
www.bromleighs.com
Great selection of traditional Bakelite fittings.

Le Klint
www.leklint.dk
A Danish classic.

Original BTC England
www.originalbtc.com
A British classic.

Rothschild & Bickers
www.rothschildbickers.com
Elegant and original lights.

Modular Lighting Instruments
www.supermodular.com
Super-stylish luminaires.

Woka Lamps Vienna
www.wokalamps.com/en
*Expensive but inspiring, especially lights
designed by Josef Frank.*

Flooring

Alternative Flooring
www.alternativeflooring.com
All natural flooring.

Dalsouple
www.dalsouple.com
Rubber flooring in endless colours.

Dinesen
www.dinesen.com

Forbo Flooring Systems
www.forbo-flooring.com
Linoleum and marmoleum.

François Gilles
www.francoisgilles.co.uk
Moreish Moorish rugs.

The Reclaimed Flooring Company
www.reclaimedflooringco.com

The Rug Company
www.therugcompany.info
Covetable rugs.

Rush Matters
www.rushmatters.co.uk
Lovely company, people and products.

Solid Floor
www.solidfloor.co.uk
Timber and resin flooring.

Hardware

Quincaillerie Belot
www.quincaillerie-belot.com

Turnstyle Designs
www.turnstyledesigns.co.uk
Everything from a doorknob to a dimmer switch.

Materials

Material Connexion
www.materialconnexion.com

Material Lab
www.material-lab.co.uk

Non-allergenic

The Healthy House Ltd
www.healthy-house.co.uk

Paint

Auro
www.auro.co.uk

Dulux
www.dulux.com
A good website featuring current trends and a virtual decorating device.

Milk Paint
www.milkpaint.com

Paper, Fabric and Leather

Amy Butler Design
www.amybutlerdesign.com
Bold fabrics and accessories inspired by big America.

Bridge of Weir Leather
www.bowleather.co.uk
Luscious products sensitively produced.

Bute
www.butefabrics.co.uk
Handsome, hardwearing and beloved.

Classic Textiles
www.classictextiles.com
Vintage prints brought back to life by The Glasgow School of Art.

Kvadrat
www.kvadrat.dk
High quality and chic.

Marimekko
www.marimekko.fi/eng/
Classic Scandinavian prints, plus much more.

Studio Printworks
www.studioprintworks.com
Rather brilliant wallpapers and fabrics.

Tapettitalo
www.tapettitalo.fi/english.html
A smorgasbord of wild wallpaper.

TREASURE TROVE

Salvage

Antique Appliances
www.antiqueappliances.com

Salvo Web
www.salvoweb.com

Urban Remains
www.urbanremainschicago.com

Sanitary and Brassware

H.M. James & Sons Ltd
www.hmjames.co.uk/colours.htm
Wonderfully coloured baths, sinks and toilets.

Victorian Plumbing
www.victorianplumbing.co.uk
*A good selection of original antique
fittings, but you do have to look.*

Tiles and Concrete

Concrete Blond
www.concrete-blond.com

Heath Ceramics
www.heathceramics.com

Upholstery

Aiveen Daly
www.aiveendaly.com
Furniture's couturier.

A few more of my favourite suppliers where
there is always something to be enchanted by:

1st Dibs
www.1stdibs.com
*'The most beautiful things on earth'…
and possibly the most expensive. but an
inspiring place to 'window shop' nevertheless.*

Anthropologie
www.anthropologie.com
*Brimming with joyful stuff for your home.
And now available both sides of the Atlantic.*

Bottles and Glashaus
www.bottles.de
*A breathtaking collection of glass
receptacles. If you are tempted, it does
help if you speak German and/or are
planning a visit to Munich.*

John Derian
www.johnderian.com
Charmingly eccentric.

Die Imaginäre Manufaktur
Oranienstraße 26, 10999 Berlin
Tel. +49 (0)30 28 50 30 121
E-Mail: dim@u-s-e.org
*Baskets and brushes made by the German
Blind Institute.*

Emery and Cie
www.emeryetcie.com
A wonderland.

H. Skjalm P.
www.hskjalmp.dk
*Charming and useful household
accessories from Denmark.*

Labour and Wait
www.labourandwait.co.uk
Sense and sensibility.

London Taxidermy
www.londontaxidermy.com
*Alexis maintains the highest standards
and a very sharp eye.*

Manufactum
www.manufactum.co.uk
*Charming and useful household
accessories from Germany.*

Michael Anastassiades
www.michaelanastassiades.com
An artist and a gent.

RE
www.re-foundobjects.com
*Once logged on to this website you may
never leave.*

Retrouvius
www.retrouvius.com
*Talented architects and designers with
a must-visit shop.*

bibliography

Creativity, design and living life to the full

☐ Bachelard, Gaston, *The Poetics of Space*
East Sussex: Beacon Press, 1969

☐ Banham, Reyner, *Theory and Design in the First Machine Age* London: Architectural Press, 1980

☐ Brue, Alexia, *Cathedrals of the Flesh: In Search of the Perfect Bath* London: Bloomsbury, 2003

☐ Cameron, Julia, *The Artist's Way* New York: Tarcher/Penguin, 1997

☐ David, Elizabeth, *An Omelette and a Glass of Wine* London: Penguin, 1986

☐ Dorst, Kees, *Understanding Design* Amsterdam: BIS Publishers, 2006

☐ Pallasmaa, Juhani, *The Eyes Of The Skin* New Jersey: John Wiley & Sons, 1996

☐ Perec, Georges, *Species of Spaces and Other Pieces* London: Penguin, 1997

☐ Potter, Norman, *What is a Designer: Things. Places. Messages.* London: Hyphen Press, 1980

☐ Tanizaki, Jun'ichiro, *In Praise of Shadows* London: Vintage, 2001

☐ Vernon, M.D., *The Psychology of Perception* London: Penguin, 1962

Practical guides

☐ Conran, Terence, *Eco House Book* London: Conran Octopus, 2009

☐ Lane, Thomas; Parikh, Anoop and Robertson, Deborah, *The Conran Octopus Decorating Book* London: Conran Octopus, 1997

☐ McCloud, Kevin, *Choosing Colours: An Expert Choice of the Best Colours to Use in Your Home* London: Quadrille, 2003

☐ Storey, Sally, *Perfect Lighting: New Tools and Techniques for Every Room in the Home* London: Jacqui Small, 2008

☐ Wolverton, B.C., *Eco-friendly Houseplants: 50 Indoor Plants That Purify the Air* London: Weidenfeld & Nicolson Illustrated, 1996

index

Italic pagination indicates illustrations

acknowledgements

The publisher would like to thank the following photographers, agencies and designers for their kind permission to reproduce the following:

3 Jean-Francois Jaussaud (Interior designer: Matali Crasset); 6 Graham Atkins-Hughes/Media 10 Images; 12 Robertino Nikolic/Artur/View Pictures; 16 Jake Curtis (Architects: FAT); 17 Lorenzo Nencioni/Vega mg (Architect: Sabrina Bignami); 20 Hotze Eisma/Taverne Agency; 22–23 Mark Williams; 24–25 Katsuhida Kida (Architects: Ushida Findlay); 27 Vincent Knapp/ Tripod Agency; 28 Gap Interiors/Inside-E.Saillet (Decoration: Stephanie Garotin, www.labergeriedefeline.com); 30 Vincent Knapp © The World of Interiors (October 2002); 31 Tim Street-Porter (Interior Designer: Steven Gambrel); 32 Richard Powers (Architect: Abigail Turin - Kallosturin, www.kallosturin.com); 33 Henry Wilson © The World of Interiors (June 2009); 34 Huntely Hedworth/Elizabeth Whiting & Associates; 36 Eric Morin © The World of Interiors (July 2009); 37 Chris Tubbs/Red Cover; 38 Michele Biancucci/The Interior Archive; 39 Jan Baldwin/Narratives; 40 left Copyright 2009 Lemon Street Gallery & Kurt Jackson. Used with permission; 41 Nathalie Krag/Taverne Agency; 42 "Hiepler, Brunier" (Architects: GRAFT); 43 Jan Bitter (Architect: GRAFT); 44 Office for Metropolitan Architecture; 54 Ngoc Minh Ngo (Designer: Betsey Johnson); 57 Christian Schaulin; 58 Grazia Ike Branco (Architect: Michael Dahmen/DDJ Architekten - Dusseldorf (D); 59 below Grazia Ike Branco (Architect: Wespi - De Meuron Architekten - Caviano (CH)); 59 above Erik Zappon/House of Pictures (Styling: Vivian Boje/House of Pictures); 61 Richard Powers (Artist: Rodrigo Bueno, www.mataadentro.com.br); 62 Conrad White/zapaimages; 63 left Lorenzo Nencioni/Vega mg (Interior Decorator: Emma Rochlitzer); 63 right Cookie Kinkead (Apartment of Designer: Barbara Hulanicki); 65 Prue Ruscoe/Taverne Agency; 66 Ben Anders; 67 above Ray Main/Mainstream Images/Smithcreative.net; 67 below Simon McBride/Red Cover; 69 Paul Massey/Red Cover; 70 above Ngoc Minh Ngo/Taverne Agency; 70 below Denise Boneneti/Vega mg; 70–71 Henry Wilson © The World of Interiors (February 2009); 73 Simon McBride/Red Cover; 74 Camera Press/MCM/Mark Eden Schooley/Marion Bayle;

75 above Pernille Kaalund/House of Pictures (Stylist: Louise Kamman Riising/House of Pictures); 75 below Svend Dyrvig (Styling: Nathalie Veil)/House of Pictures; 77 Miguel Flores Vianna/The Interior Archive; 78 Ray Main/Mainstream Images/Arne Maynard; 79 above left Marita Jonsson; 79 above right John Dummer/Taverne Agency; 79 below Simon McBride/Red Cover; 81 Beth Evans; 82 above left Ben Anders; 82 above right Giulio Oriani/Vega mg; 82 below Mark Luscombe-Whyte/The Interior Archive; 83 Ngoc Minh Ngo (Designer: Thomas Paul); 86–87 Courtesy of Dinesen (Project designed by Signe Bindslev Henriksen. Dinesen Douglas floorboards); 88 left Gaelle Le Boulicaut (Stylist: Jeremy Callaghan, Architect: Atelier Serre Fernandez); 88–89 Rachael Smith (Geoff Powell, www.rethinkyourhome.com); 90 Guy Bouchet; 91 Rachael Smith (Carolyn Sceales design); 92–93 Paul Raeside/Living Etc/IPC+; 93 above Paul Ryan-Goff/Red Cover (Architect: Kastrup & Sjunnesson); 93 below Richard Powers (Donna Karen International www.dkny.com; Architects: Bonetti Kozerski www.bonettikozerski.com); 94 Mel Yates/Media 10 Images (Architect: David Mikhail); 95 Nathalie Krag/Taverne Agency; 96 left Simon Upton/The Interior Archive; 96 right James Mitchell/Living Etc/IPC+; 97 Rachael Smith (Geoff Powell, www.rethinkyourhome.com); 98 above Jake Curtis/Living Etc/IPC+; 98 below Ray Main/ Mainstream Images/Architect: Seth Stein; 98–99 Ray Main/Mainstream Images/Design www.juliabarnard.co.uk; 100 Ray Main/Mainstream Images/Design: Echodesign.co.uk; 101 left Bernard Touillon/Cote Sud/Camera Press; 101 right Mads Mogensen; 102 Martin Dyrløv/House of Pictures (Styling: Lene Samsø/House of Pictures); 103 Emma Lee/Narratives; 104–105 Åke E:Son Lindman (Architects: Hans Murman/Ulla Alberts, Murman Arkitekter); 106 left Chris Tubbs/Red Cover; 106–107 Grazia Ike Branco (Architect: Michael Dahmen/DDJ Architekten - Dusseldorf (D); 107 centre Henry Wilson © The World of Interiors (February 2009); 107 right Jean-Francois Jaussaud (Interior designer: Stella Cadente); 108 Camera Press/MCM/Mai-Linh/C.Ardouin/Abigail Ahern, decorator; 109 left Gaelle Le Boulicaut (Stylist: Jeremy Callaghan, Architect; Alex Michaelis); 109 right Jake Curtis/Living

Etc/IPC+; 110 above Sarah Blee/OWI; 110 below Catherine Gratwicke; 111 VERNE, production Hilde Bouchez/OWI; 112 Richard Powers (Architect: Marmol Radziner, www.marmol-radziner.com); 113 Ed Reeve (Architect: David Adjaye); 114 Sean Myers/Media 10 Images (Architect and homeowner: Luke Tozer of Pitman Tozer); 115 above Alexander van Berge; 115 below Reto Guntli/zapaimages; 116 left Lorenzo Nencioni/Vega mg; 116-117 Jan Baldwin/Narratives (Home of artists Erica Van Horn and Simon Cutts (Coracle Press); 118 above Paul Massey/Living Etc/IPC+; 118 below Jefferson Smith/Media 10 Images (Architect and homeowner: Jack Bonnington); 119 above Camera Press/MCM/Mai-Linh/Box Management/Catherine Ardouin/Architect: Marco Costanzi; 119 below Birgitta Wolfgang Drejer/Sisters Agency; 120 Martin Lof; 121 Camera Press/MCM/P.Lepreux/D.Rozensztroch/C.Tiné; 122 Verity Welstead/ Narratives; 123 left Richard Powers (Architect: Marmol Radziner, www.marmol-radziner.com); 123 right Jan Baldwin/Narratives (Home of artists Erica Van Horn and Simon Cutts (Coracle Press); 124 above Richard Powers (Architects: Robertson & Hindmarsh, www.robertsonhindmarsh.com.au); 124 below Minh+Wass; 125 left Nathalie Krag/Taverne Agency; 125 right Chris Tubbs/Red Cover; 127 Julian Wass (Designers: Mary Cooper & Tomio Thomann); 128 left Mel Yates/Media 10 Images (Architect and homeowner: Suzanne Brewer); 128–129 Xavier Béjot/Tripod Agency; 130 Paul Raeside/LIving Etc/IPC+; 131 above left Birgitta Wolfgang Drejer/Sisters Agency; 131 below left Agi Simoes/zapaimages (Interior Designer: Sue Rohrer); 131 right Alun Callender/Red Cover; 132 Filip Dujardin/OWI; 133 Gaelle Le Boulicaut (Stylist: Allan James Stuart, Architect: Xavier Clarós); 134 Gaelle Le Boulicaut (Stylist: Allan James Stuart, Architect: Xavier Clarós); 135 above left Camera Press; 135 above right Heidi Lerkenfeldt/Linnea Press (Stylist: Pernille Vest); 135 below Melanie Acevedo; 136–137 Chris Tubbs/ Media 10 Images (Architect and homeowner: Alex Michaelis); 137 above right Mads Mogensen; 137 below left Camera Press/Marie Claire Maison/Gregoire Vieille/Delphine Fromental; 137 below right Ditte Isager/Taverne Agency; 138 above left Jan Baldwin/Narratives (Architect: Kay Hartmann); 138 below left Jason Schmidt; 138–139 Richard Powers (Architect: techentin buckingham architecture, inc., www.techbuckarch.com); 140 left VERNE, production Hilde Bouchez/OWI; 140 right Jean Pierre Gabriel/OWI (Designer: Jules Wabbes); 141 left Henry Wilson/Red Cover; 141 right Simon McBride/Red Cover; 142 left Richard Powers (Design: Jacob Blom); 142–143 Graham Atkins-Hughes/Red Cover; 144 Chris Tubbs; 145 Henry Wilson © The World of Interiors (February 2009); 146 Jan Baldwin/Narratives; 147 above Birgitta Wolfgang Drejer/Sisters Agency; 147 below left Richard Powers (Design: Kevin Haley, www.kevinhaley.com); 147 below rightPaul Massey/Living Etc/IPC+; 148 Simon Upton/The Interior Archive; 150 above Chris Tubbs/Red Cover; 150 below Gaelle Le Boulicaut (Stylist: Jeremy Callaghan, Architect; Alex Michaelis); 151 Hotze Eisma/Taverne Agency; 152–153 Beto Consorte/ Triptyque; 153 above Jan Baldwin/Narratives; 153 below Gap Interiors/Inside/J.Hall (Architect: Page Goolrick); 154 Thomas Stewart/Media 10 Images (Architect: Architect: Willson & Bell); 155 above left Hanna Dlugosz/Vega mg (Architect: Moto Architekki & PVKO Architects); 155 above right Camera Press/Marie Claire Maison/Jerome Galland/Aleph/Delphine Fromental; 156 Camera Press/Marie Claire Maison/Jerome Galland/Aleph; 158 Andreas von Einsiedel (Interior Designer: Emmanuel Garcin); 159 above Jan Baldwin/ Narratives (Architect: Jonathan Clark, www.jonathanclark.co.uk); 159 below Gap Interiors/Inside/W. Waldron (Interior Designer: Barry Rice); 160 above Ben Anders; 160 below Beth Evans; 164 Per Magnus Persson/House of Pictures (Styling: Jimmie Schønning/House of Pictures); 167 Kyle Alexander/ Collection: Workbook stock/Getty Images; 168–169 Camera Press/Cote Sud/Gilles Trillard; 170 left Ngoc Minh Ngo (Designer: Daniel Jasiak); 170 right Chris Tubbs/Red Cover; 171 Courtesy of Dinesen (Project designed by Lars Gitz Architects. Dinesen Douglas floorboards; 173 Mirjam Bleeker (Production: Frank Visser); 174 Ray Main/Mainstream/ Andrew Weaving/20th Century Design; 175 Hotze Eisma/Taverne Agency;176 Gaelle Le Boulicaut (Stylist: Jeremy Callaghan); 177 Richard Powers (Interior Architect: Albano Daminato, www.albanodaminato.com); ; 178 above left A. Ianniello/Studiopep (Stylist: Petra Barkhof);

178 above right Mel Yates/Media 10 Images (Architect and homeowner: Sarah Featherstone); 178 below left Simon Upton/The Interior Archive; 178 below right Camera Press/Maison Française/Anne Françoise Pelissier; 180 Ponti Brown by Suzanne Sharp at The Rug Company; 181 Winfried Heinze/Red Cover (Interior Designer: Lisa Weeks, Furniture Designer: Amy Somerville); 182 left Crown Inn - brand concept and design by Studioilse. Photography: Lisa Cohen. Flooring by Rush Matters; 182 right Richard Powers (Architect: Arthur Casas, www.arthurcasas.com); 183 Bill Amberg/The Communications Store; 184–185 Nathalie Krag/Taverne Agency; 186 Gaelle Le Boulicaut (Stylist: Anne Pericchi Draeger, Architect: Burrati Battiston www.burattibattiston.it); 187 above Warren Smith/Red Cover; 187 below left Thomas Stewart/Media 10 Images (Wallpaper: Trine Anderson - Ferm Living); 187 below right Mike Daines/Red Cover; 188–189 above Andreas von Einsiedel (Architecture and Design: Matteo Thun); 188–189 below Camera Press/Marie Claire Maison/Gilles de Chabeneix/Jean-Pascal Billaud; 189 right Jake Curtis/Living Etc/IPC+; 190 left Richard Powers (Design: Melissa Collison, www.melissacollison.com.au); 190–191 Lisa Cohen/Taverne Agency; 191 right Andreas von Einsiedel (Interior Designer: David Carter); 192 left Xavier Béjot /Tripod Agency; 192 above right Jefferson Smith/Media 10 Images; 192 below right Gaelle Le Boulicaut (Stylist: Jeremy Callaghan, Architect: Rudi Riccioti, Interior architect: Nicola & Adelaide Marchi); 194 Gaelle Le Boulicaut (Stylist: Allan James Stuart); 195 Camera Press/ACP/Derek Swalwell; 196–197 Paul Raeside/Mainstream Images; 198–199 Hotze Eisma/Taverne Agency;); 200 above Gaelle Le Boulicaut (Stylist: Jeremy Callaghan, Architect: Sam Marshall); 200 below Jan Baldwin/Narratives (Architect: Jonathan Clark, www.jonathanclark.co.uk; 201 above Camera Press; 201 below A.Mezza & E. Escalante/Narratives; 202 left John Dummer/Taverne Agency; 202 centre Frederik Vercruysse/OWI (Production & Stylist: Kat de Baerdemaeker/OWI, Architect: Karel Vandenhende); 202 right Marjon Hoogervorst/ Taverne Agency; 203 Rachael Smith (www.kearsley.co.uk); 204 Andrea Ferrari; 205 Camera Press/Maison/ Frederic Ducout; 206 Palomba Collection from Laufen Ltd (Designed by Ludovica and Roberto

Palomba); 207 Deborah Jaffe; 208–209 Frederik Vercruysse/OWI (Interior: An Oost); 209 above Andreas von Einsiedel (Interior Designer: Bruno Raymond); 209 below left Ray Main/Mainstream Images/Designer: Ou Baholyodhin; 209 below right Naomi Cleaver; 210 left Hotze Eisma/Taverne Agency; 210 right Chris Tubbs/Red Cover; 211 Mark Luscombe-Whyte/The Interior Archive; 212–213 Ben Anders; 214 A.Mezza & E. Escalante/ Narratives; 215 Camera Press/Marie Claire Maison/Philippe Garcia; 216 Paul Massey/Living Etc/IPC+; 217 Ray Main/ Mainstream/Andrew Weaving/20th Century Design; 218–219 Rachael Smith (www.kearsley.co.uk); 220 Damian Russell; 221 Reto Guntli/zapaimages (Interior Designer: Tony Ingrao); 224 Jan Baldwin/ Narratives (Architect: Jonathan Clark, www.jonathanclark.co.uk); 226 Jefferson Smith/ Media 10 Images (Architect: Richard Paxton & Mooarc); 227 left Jake Fitzjones/Living Etc/IPC+; 227 right Gaelle Le Boulicaut (Stylist: Jeremy Callaghan, Architect: Nathalie Wolberg); 228 above Jefferson Smith/Media 10 Images (Architect & Developer: Edgley Design); 228 below Edina van der Wyck/ Media 10 Images (Architect: Powell Tuck Associates); 229 Emma Lee/Media 10 Images (Naomi Cleaver's House); 230 Dan Duchars/Living Etc/IPC+; 231 Bob Smith/Living Etc/IPC+; 232–233 Jake Curtis/ Living Etc/IPC+; 233 Giorgio Possenti/Vega mg (Architects: Carlo Donati); 234 Mel Yates/Media 10 Images (Architect and homeowner: Suzanne Brewer); 235 Paul Massey/Mainstream Images/ naomicleaver.com; 236 Gap Interiors/Inside/H&L/ E. Young; 237 A. Ianniello/Studiopep (Interior Designer: Paolo Badesco, Stylist: Petra Barkhof); 238 Ray Main/Mainstream Images; 239 Hotze Eisma/Taverne Agency; 242–243 Darren Chung/ Mainstream Images/ Hemingway Design; 252–253 Mel Yates/Living Etc/IPC+; 260–261 Xavier Béjot /Tripod Agency; 264 Courtesy of Emery & Cie; 268–269 Jan Baldwin/ Narratives; 276–277 Paul Massey/Living Etc/IPC+; 284 VERNE (Production: Hilde Bouchez)/OWI (Artist: Vladimir Kagan and Erica Wilson); 304 Hans Zeegers/ Taverne Agency

Every effort has been made to trace the copyright holders. We apologise in advance for any unintentional omissions and would be pleased to insert the appropriate acknowledgment in any subsequent publication.

I would like to thank: Kathleen Hall, my dear friend and right hand woman, without whose indefatigable support, particularly in managing our UK studio, I would not have been able to shut myself away and write this book.

Maya Vuksa, Caroline Jackson, Kitty Nunneley, Ruth Dalziell, Peter Lazarus at Carpet Solutions, Ed Reeve, Richard Thompson, Alan Fox at Turgon Flooring, Piers and Rory at Designers Block, Tim Francis at Tea London and Holger Jacobs at Mind Design, for their observations and assistance.

All the people from whom I have learnt about building and homes over the years (and continue to learn from) including my family, my tutors, the architects and designers I have worked with, especially Steve Jensen at Anarchitect; the TV and newspaper teams I have worked with; the many and varied contractors and sub contractors I have built with and, most importantly, my clients.

The magical Caribbean island of Nevis that provided the perfect writing environment.

Bombay Sapphire gin and Oreo cookies, which provided essential refreshments.

KBJ, for doing the business so beautifully, as always.

Conran Octopus, but most especially Lorraine Dickey, Sybella Marlow, Jonathan Christie, Liz Boyd and Alison Wormleighton – for the joy of it all.

And my beloved husband Oliver, most particularly his catering and housekeeping skills, big strong arms and inspiring mind without which I simply would not have been able to write about the joy of home.